SCARS OF THE SOUL
ARE WHY KIDS WEAR BANDAGES
WHEN THEY DON'T HAVE BRUISES

SCARS OF THE SOUL
ARE WHY KIDS WEAR BANDAGES
WHEN THEY DON'T HAVE BRUISES

MILES MARSHALL LEWIS

Akashic Books
New York

Published by Akashic Books
©2004 Miles Marshall Lewis

"Another Great Day in Harlem" originally appeared in *XXL* under the title "Hip Hop America"; "Notes Toward a Hiphop Politik" originally appeared in *The Nation* (in shorter form) under the title "Russell Simmons's Rap"; "Spelmo Babies and Other Bourgeois Ephemera" originally appeared in *L.A. Weekly* (in shorter form) under the title "All About the Benjamins."

ISBN: 1-888451-71-8
Library of Congress Control Number: 2004106235
All rights reserved
First printing
Printed in Canada

Akashic Books
PO Box 1456
New York, NY 10009
Akashic7@aol.com
www.akashicbooks.com
www.milesmarshalllewis.com

CONTENTS

Preface   11

I. MEMORY LANES, GUN HILL ROADS
Bronx Science   19
Famous Negro Writer #77   41
The Suckerpunch of My Childhood Files   53
Mama's Gun   63
Worldwide Underground   71

II. THE DEF OF HIPHOP
Peace, Unity, Love, Having Fun   81
Notes Toward a Hiphop Politik   109
Spelmo Babies and Other Bourgeois Ephemera   135
Go Make of All Disciples   149
Scars of the Soul Are Why Kids Wear Bandages
   When They Don't Have Bruises   173
Another Great Day in Harlem   189

Acknowledgments   199

To my mother and my father.

And to the sons of '70,
and the spirit of '88.

Fresh for '04 . . . you suckas!

HIPHOP IS DEAD.
Writing *Scars of the Soul Are Why Kids Wear Bandages When They Don't Have Bruises,* I worked backwards from this foregone conclusion, then changed my opinion very early on. Living in the South Bronx at the time hiphop culture was born, moving to the northeast Bronx neighborhood of Co-op City and seeing things progress as a youngster, I had become disillusioned by the turn of the millennium, and I was not alone. A hot topic of debate for those of us who have seen the culture's better days, many missives on the death of hiphop float through cyberspace even now. *The Source* magazine questioned, "Who is killing the spirit of hiphop?" at a Harvard hiphop town hall meeting moderated by the Reverend Al Sharpton, which I attended in December 2000. Interviewing Q-Tip in February 2002 concerning an album on which he'd largely abandoned rhyming and rap arrangements, the renowned MC shared my opinion. "I can faithfully, honestly say that hiphop is dead and it follows the route of all other forms of black music," he said. "I'm really ashamed of the state it's in right now."

Hiphop as a culture and art form graduated from subculture status during the early 1990s, significantly figuring in the lives of worldwide youth and ending its standing as an underground phenomenon. With its mainstream success came more radio-friendly beats and rhymes, and certain characteristics that appealed to its wider audience were forefronted: crass bling-bling materialism; violent rap rivalries that extended beyond records into real-life shootings, stabbings, and murders; the objectification and denigration of women in videos and song lyrics. Furthermore, most modern rap music aficionados had no appreciation for aerosol art, deejaying, or breaking—sidelined aspects of hiphop culture whose former prominence I remembered fondly from the seventies and early eighties. I began to embrace more of a post-hiphop aesthetic, as if a new youth subculture was right around the corner and hiphop was on its deathbed.

Around the same time I became reacquainted with my old elementary/junior-high classmate John Reed. Beginning in September 2001, corresponding from Eastern New York Correctional Facility, John began writing me about our mutual Bronx childhood and the sad state of hiphop. John Reed is worthy of his own chapter in this book, his own autobiography really. He began tagging Dazer at the age of nine, in a Co-op City tenement-building elevator with respected artists Ex-Con and Presweet. He founded his own graffiti posse, the T.V. Crew ("T.V." for The Vandals) with Maze, Stuff, Cashier, and Zent—all junior-high classmates of ours. John Reed threw up tags with local Co-op City legends like Echo and Med before beginning to rhyme as the Almighty Cool Jay in 1982, years prior to the debut of LL Cool J. By then he had also begun to study the Five Percenter doctrines of the Nation of Gods and Earths, a more militant offshoot of the Nation of Islam popular during the eighties; John Reed became Justice Allah. As the Almighty Cool Jay he founded an MC crew dubbed the Funky Fresh 3—later the original Fresh 3 MCs—with my tweener acquaintances Harry Dee and Ice Ice. In 1982 John Reed's older brother Mark disbanded his own MC crew, Playboys Inc., and started a new group; they battled the Fresh 3 MCs for the rights to their name and won, releasing the popular rap single "Fresh" months later on Profile Records. Undaunted, John Reed launched the Boogie Down Breakers, capitalizing on his skills as a stunt roller-skater and breaker at Bronx spots like White Plains Road's original Skate Key. He would go on to battle and defeat the popular breaker Popatron, all this before the age of thirteen. This is the hiphop lifestyle that makes us sentimental.

A few words from John Reed—January 26, 2004, from Clinton Correctional Center in Dannemora, New York:

Eighth grade was a special time for me. Especially the end of the school year, 1984. I remember I.S. 180's eighth grade prom. I wore all white. White Lees with the permanent crease, white Chams de Baron shirt, white on white Adidas with white fat laces, white band gloves, a long white scarf that hung over my neck like Tyson wore his heavyweight belts, a white Kangol hat with Section Five's five popular letters ironed on the front: F.R.E.S.H. Also, a name-buckle with JAY and a medallion and chain. Rather than being like everybody else who rented limousines or walked to the prom, I was chauffeured by Sha-Born. I was on the front of his bike handlebars from Section Five to the front door of 180. Everybody was outside checking out each other and I pulled up on the front of the bike with Sha-Born pedaling hard and as we planned, Sha-Born hit the brakes and I flew off the bike (another stunt) into the crowd and just started dancing. Everybody cheered, clapped, laughed, and the haters/admirers just grinned and shook their heads.

The prom ended with a breaking battle in our cafeteria; John won and walked off with Liticia Padilla a/k/a Bunny Tee, one of the finest girls in the eighth grade. He was what you might call a ghetto celebrity, one of the neighborhood superstars. In adulthood he joined the Nation of Islam as John Muhammad, moving to the South Bronx with his wife. When she was robbed at gunpoint in 1993 he tracked her assailant down and stabbed him in the leg, an accidental murder. John fled police for five months before turning himself in. Sentenced in 1994 to twelve-to-twenty-five years for manslaughter in the first degree, John is eligible for parole in 2006.

"[I]n our official seal you will see the year 1970. This is when *we* begin modern Hiphop. We arrived at this year knowing that Kool DJ Herc (the recognized father of Hip Hop) began playing music in the parks of the Bronx, New York, around 1972 and Afrika Bambaataa of Zulu Nation (the recognized godfather of Hip Hop) begins Hiphop in November 1974. Although Hiphop's true origin date remains a mystery, the Temple of Hiphop begins modern Hiphop in the year 1970 for teaching purposes. Not only does this year close the period in which some of the first generation of Hiphoppas were born (1961–1971), but it was throughout the 1970s (1971–1981) that modern Hiphop came into physical existence."

—*The Gospel of Hiphop*

BEGINNING THIS BOOK with "Bronx Science," I aimed beyond documenting the social atomization of hiphop alone and decided on creating an essay collection revealing of my own life as a child of the culture. With the novel

Midnight's Children, Salman Rushdie told the story of Saleem Sinai, a character born at the stroke of midnight on August 15, 1947, the precise moment that India gained its independence. The course of Sinai's life was inextricably linked to his nation's disasters and triumphs in Rushdie's fictional account. Being born in 1970 and raised in the Bronx—like hiphop culture itself—I chose to document facets of my wonder years as inextricably linked to the hiphop nation in the opening "Memory Lanes, Gun Hill Roads" section.

My correspondence with John Muhammad was essential to the creation of this book, reminding me of what we'd experienced as Bronx-born adolescents in the eye of newborn hiphop's storm. Exchanging letters with John Muhammad, coupled with my disenchantment with rap music, inspired me to pen essays that dealt with the condition of hiphop culture and my visceral childhood connections with it.

In 2004, the thirtieth anniversary of hiphop culture, I wanted to capture the spirit of its three-decade history by telling some Bronx tales, my own in particular. "The Def of Hiphop" section concerns hiphop institutions like the Universal Zulu Nation, the Hiphop Summit Action Network, and the Temple of Hiphop, all working toward the benefit and furtherance of the culture. I drew the conclusion that hiphop's alive and well largely because of those organizations' efforts, reversing my initial position due in part also to the reasoned arguments laid out in "Scars of the Soul Are Why Kids Wear Bandages When They Don't Have Bruises," the title essay. Not every selection in this volume deals with the thesis of hiphop's coming apart, but all reflect my nostalgic yet post-hiphop mood at the time of these writings.

Hiphop is not dead but it's got some issues, and I felt it

best to address and explore these issues in a context of compassion rather than wash my hands of the whole thing. Which would be impossible for me anyway. I am hiphop.

Miles Marshall Lewis
Harlem, New York
September 2004

I. MEMORY LANES, GUN HILL ROADS

BRONX SCIENCE

"In Samuel 4:21, Eli's daughter-in-law names her son Ichabod, saying, 'The glory is departed from Israel.' Ichabod is a disappointed word for disappointment. My favorite kind of scribblers are ichabods. To be an ichabod is to be a nostalgia artist. Let the Futurists do their thing, let the ichabods do theirs."

—Zadie Smith

NEIGHBORS IN MY MOTHER'S BUILDING were accustomed to the police. Officers had responded to the particular domestic disturbance calls of 15B on eight occasions since the couple's marriage three years ago, resulting in two temporary orders of protection for Kerri Flowers and one conviction on a second-degree harassment charge brought against my old fourth grade classmate Derek Slade. Several years ago cops were summoned to their Bronx home three times in three days. At two-thirty in the morning on the last of these three calls, two officers followed a sergeant down the corridor toward the sound of a wailing three-month-old baby and the communication-breakdown clamor unique to marital strain. Kerri Flowers stormed to answer the doorbell; her husband closed the door of the bedroom they once shared. Chilled air flooded the room as an agitated

Derek Slade opened the window, lifted his infant son for the final time, and flung young Kharel Chamar Slade fifteen stories to his death.

"Where's my baby!" Kerri Flowers shouted. "Where's my baby!"

The police entered the bedroom as the mother frantically searched a closet for her only child, her husband handcuffed for violating an order of protection. An officer quickly assessed the rolled-up baby blanket on the bed, the window still open to the October cold. Kerri Flowers reached the window first.

"My baby!" Kerri Flowers screamed through tears. "You killed my baby!"

The sergeant dashed out of the bedroom, out of the apartment, racing down fifteen flights of stairs. One officer restrained Kerri Flowers as the other asked Derek Slade in furious disbelief if he had actually thrown his son through the open window.

"Yeah, I did," Derek Slade answered calmly. "I knew I shouldn't have done it," he would later tell detectives at the Forty-fifth Precinct stationhouse. "If I wasn't going to have my son, no one was." On the spot, the sergeant arrested and charged Derek Slade—rechristened Shakem Allah by the Nation of Gods and Earths back when we were teenagers at Harry S. Truman High School—with second-degree murder, first-degree manslaughter, and second-degree criminal contempt. In Bronx Criminal Court the following morning Derek Slade plead not guilty.

Officers located baby Kharel Slade face-up in a flowerbed wearing a diaper and a T-shirt, in front of the same building where an assailant raped my ex-girlfriend's teenage sister in 1994. Kharel Slade was pronounced dead from blunt trauma to the head outside 140 Debs Place at two-forty-five, October 17, 2000. Derek Slade last kissed his son sometime after eight o'clock the night before, kissed him goodbye as he packed a bag to take back to 2420 Hunter Avenue where he was staying with family members elsewhere in Co-op City. When Derek Slade returned at two A.M. with his own front-door key he soon became enraged by passionate resentments against his estranged wife. Kerri Flowers startled awake; Derek Slade lifted his son from slumber and began feeding the child, who was sick from a common cold.

As Kerri Flowers exited the bedroom, Derek Slade opened a window. "Don't tell me how to be a father!" he burst out after his child's mother suggested he close the window in light of their baby's cold. Kerri Flowers had already phoned 911. Following this first strike, husband and wife relaunched the war of words that first began shortly after their 1997 marriage, awaking neighbors, until police buzzed the inter-com from the lobby at two twenty-six.

"He knew that Kharel meant everything to Kerri," remarked a neighbor, "that she adored him, that her baby meant the world to her. Whatever problems they may have been having, Kerri said she never thought he would do any-thing to harm their baby. But the baby's father was jealous of Kharel because all Kerri's love was going to their son. He did this to hurt Kerri and he just crushed her whole world."

"She tried and tried to be a family," said a childhood friend, "and she thought that the baby would finally make them a family. He said he wanted a child and he acted like he wanted a child but he didn't. You can't be a family by killing your baby. She didn't want to be with him anymore and he knew the only way he could hurt her would be through the baby. And he did. He crushed her."

Detectives arrived, some shedding tears as they covered the lifeless body of Kharel Slade with a sheet. Officers guided Kerri Flowers, sobbing, downstairs and into a squad car. Compounding this catastrophic personal tragedy was the recent death of her grandmother and losing her father to colon cancer just months earlier. "I don't think I'll ever forget her cries last night," said a neighbor. "It was a sound that tore through your heart." The squad car delivered Kerri Flowers to Jacobi Medical Center where she was treated for shock and sedated. Residents of Co-op City peered from windows and stood on terraces staring at the scene. Some minds were no doubt transported to the events of the previous Thursday when a fifteen-year-old boy stabbed his mother to death over cutting class at Truman High, in a building across from my own grandmother's. Minutes later officers corralled Derek Slade into another squad car. Judge John A. Barone arraigned him on murder charges and ordered him held without bail at Bronx Criminal Court.

Legendary jazz bandleader Edward "Duke" Ellington (1899–1974) rests eternally beside trumpeter Sir Miles Dewey Davis III (1926–1991) in the northeast Bronx at Woodlawn Cemetery, a little-known fact. Vibes player Lionel Hampton (1908–2002) was also interred there recently. The youngest to be buried at Woodlawn, in a plot donated by the cemetery, is Kharel Chamar Slade (July 20, 2000–October 17, 2000), the late son of my old homeboy from elementary school.

I WAS BORN IN 1970, the year Melvin Van Peebles directed *Sweet Sweetback's Baadasssss Song* and Toni Morrison published *The Bluest Eye,* the year Afrika Bambaataa began to deejay. From the window of my apartment on Sugar Hill in Harlem I can presently catch sight of incandescent lights brightening Yankee Stadium some five thousand feet away in the Bronx. I was raised in the Highbridge section of the South Bronx—38 Marcy Place—until my parents became one of the first families to move north into Co-op City in 1974—to 120 Elgar Place. I came of age eight miles from the Sparkle at 1590 Jerome Avenue where GrandWizzard Theodore cut up "Johnny the Fox Meets Jimmy the Weed" by Thin Lizzy, thereby inventing the scratch technique, three miles from the Big 3 Barbershop where my uncle's homeboy cut hair with his pops (the shop's owner) and Slick Rick would come in for an occasional fade, two miles from where Slick Rick actually lives on Baychester Avenue, six miles from the hospitals Woody Allen and Louis Farrakhan were born in, eight miles from William H. Taft High School where Stanley Kubrick studied, five miles from where James Baldwin and Richard Avedon toiled away at the DeWitt Clinton High School magazine *The Magpie*, seven miles from where Jack Kerouac earned his football scholarship to Horace Mann High School, five miles from the Mount Saint Michael's Academy that Sean Combs attended, some railroad tracks and a greenway away from the 6 train at Pelham Bay Park which I frequently rode into Manhattan (Jennifer Lopez would hop on five stops later at Castle Hill Avenue), buildings away from where Kurtis Blow and hiphop historian Davey D and Queen Latifah and Tigger of BET's *Rap City* and Jarobi White from A Tribe Called Quest all lived in Co-op City, directly across from the tenement building of Born Unique Allah, one of the Fresh 3 MCs who recorded "Fresh." (Apologies to E. B. White.)

The world at large began its relationship with hiphop in July 1979, with the release of "Rapper's Delight" by the Sugarhill Gang, yet hiphop ceased being a purely cultural construct once it became available for sale. My own relationship with hiphop began a bit earlier, a melting Italian icee dripping down my fingers as Kool DJ AJ spun records in St. Mary's Park during the summer of 1978. The sounds of songs like "Take Me to the Mardi Gras" by Bob James and the Incredible Bongo Band's "Apache" seemed deafening even across the street from the ninth-floor window of 550

Cauldwell Avenue, my grandmother's building. When my uncle Craig—merely six years my senior—went downstairs to shoot skellies or to visit friends with fresh new platters like the *Saturday Night Fever* soundtrack, my grandmother often sent me along. So it was that summer afternoon when my curiosity about the commotion in St. Mary's Park collided with Craig's social plans to meet with his crew. I, naturally, wanted to return upstairs five minutes after arriving. Kool DJ AJ—immortalized by Kurtis Blow six years later on "AJ Scratch"—had skills, but not enough to maintain the attention of a seven-year-old weaned on Marvel Comics, Channel 5 karate movies, and *Courageous Cat and Minute Mouse*.

The following list of the gangs in the immediate South Bronx area circa the early seventies is by no means exhaustive: Black Ivory. The Black Assassins. The Black Spades. The Black Pearls. The Shades of Black. The Black Cats Inc. The Black Skulls. The Spanish Skulls. The Savage Skulls. The Savage Nomads. The Savage Samurais. The Young Samurais. The Baby Samurais. The Puerto Rican Bros. The Dynamite Bros. The Ghetto Brothers. The Brothers and Sisters. The Dominican Lions. The Spanish Daggers. Latin Aces. The Latin Kings. The Spanish Kings. The Baby Kings. The Soul Bachelors. The Cypress Bachelors. The Secret and Imperial Bachelors. The Supreme Bachelors. The Royal Javelins. The Royal Charmers. The Royal Dutchmen. The Royal Swords. The Royal Knights. The Roman Kings. The Seven Crowns. The Seven Immortals. The Young Sinners. The Young Spades. The Young Saigons. The Jolly Stompers. The Dirty Dozen. The Imperial Dutchman. The Liberated Panthers. The Majestic Warlocks. The Brothers of Satan. Born to Raise Hell. The Evil Serpents. The Slicks. The Vampires. The Dragons. The Mongols. The Undertakers. The United Lords. The Flaming Lords. The Reapers. The Renegades. The Turbans. The Henchmen. The Slices. The Peacemakers.

The Deserters. InterCrime. Power. The Casanovas. The Ching-a-Lings.

Sometime before the birth of these gangs, before my own birth even, both sides of my family had already paved inroads into the Bronx. My parents met in Harlem as proverbial high school sweethearts during the 1960s. My father's grandparents, the Johnsons, relocated north to Harlem from Georgia in the 1940s. Great-grandpa Johnson's sister had married a reverend who owned a brownstone on Findlay Avenue in the Morrisania section of the South Bronx; my great-grandparents moved in upstairs in 1969. (Come 1978, my great-grandparents relocated again to 443 St. Anns Avenue, in the Mott Haven neighborhood of Grandmaster Flash.) My mother's parents, the Bentons, were raised in Virginia (Grandma Benton) and Georgia (Grandpa Benton); they migrated to Harlem in their teens and briefly raised my mother there before mortgaging an attached row house in the northern Baychester section of the Bronx in 1965. Ninety-five percent of the times I climbed into the backseat of my parents' dung-colored Mercury Comet as a young child we were on our way to somewhere else within the borough, visiting relatives.

It seems in retrospect an inevitability that the late twentieth century—a postmodern age of flourishing irony—would spawn the global multibillion-dollar industry of hiphop from the bombed-out South Bronx. No finer example of an inner-city wasteland existed on the national map in the mid-seventies. While cousins pushed me on playground swings in Claremont Park during sunlit days, Johnny Carson targeted my great-grandparents' neighborhood for the butt of downward-spiral New York jokes on the *Tonight Show* way past my bedtime. I recall television commercials for *Fort Apache–The Bronx* and *The Warriors* (a campy favorite of my generation featuring a Coney Island gang's escape from the borough),

Hollywood films that reinforced the popular notion of the area as barren, devastated, and dangerous. Mario Merola, a Bronx County district attorney in 1973, accounts for five thousand burned-out, dilapidated South Bronx buildings in his memoir, *Big City D.A.*:

There were a lot of ways the arson game was played. The landlords who burned their property for profit often followed a pattern. First, they got the tenants on the upper floors, especially in the top rear apartments, to move out of the building. Then they would hire someone for a few bucks, maybe a kid in the neighborhood, and have him pour gasoline or some other accelerant through holes drilled in the roof and light the fire. Once the roof went, the building was considered unprofitable. Then came the profit: insurance money, sometimes a lot more than the building was worth; government funding to purchase the site from the landlord or help him rebuild; a virtual tax pardon—no law said that property taxes had to be paid out of the proceeds. Is it any wonder that most of the torched buildings were in tax arrears? And is it any wonder that we had burned-out buildings and empty lots all over the place?

Then there were those tenants who burned their own buildings so they could collect welfare money. There were also tenants who burned themselves out because they wanted to leave their privately owned tenements and move into better-maintained public housing. Fire victims always went to the top of the waiting lists for apartments in city projects.

There were scavengers who wanted to clear out buildings so they could strip them of their valuable plumbing and construction materials. There were people who set fires on the lower floors of buildings so they could burglarize top-floor apartments while the buildings were being evacuated. There were youths who simply liked to vandalize other people's property. There were social activists who believed that burning out a neighborhood would force the government to pay attention to their group's needs. There were kids who set fires because they enjoyed seeing the fire engines roll by and were caught up in the media excitement of the arson wave. There were pyromaniacs who did it for sexual thrill. And, of course, there were the common criminals who set fires to spite, frighten, to extort, to kill. Because so few arsonists are actually caught, no one knows which kind of criminal sets the most fires.

Imagine the pining sensation of nostalgia you feel skimming through the old photo album of a distant relative, bringing yourself into focus within a past context of people, places, and events blurry to your mind's eye. *Summer of Sam* evokes that feeling in my gut. The Spike Lee film detailed the summertime of 1977 from a vantage I share as a kid from the Bronx. Televised newscasts and *Daily News* headlines recounted the murderous mission of the .44 Caliber Killer, the Son of Sam. Yonkers night stalker David Berkowitz—a one-time Co-op City resident—terrorized the Bronx for a full year, claiming fifteen casualties before his August 10 arrest.

The most I have ever cared about baseball stems from that season's World Series (the New York Yankees vs. the Los Angeles Dodgers) and Reggie Jackson's historic three home runs securing the pennant for the Bronx Bombers. The Great Blackout of 1977 struck as I returned from the borough's Orchard Beach with my family, showering off sand at Grandma Benton's house. I still remember sitting on her porch and surveying the neighborhood, the candles and flashlights, the bricks through windows and "Christmas in the ghetto" looting. *Star Wars* was the talk of my first grade class, the most amazing movie we'd ever seen. (For many in that pre-cable, pre-VCR era, it was the *only* movie we'd ever seen.) As President Gerald Ford refused economic aid to the city—the *Daily News* reported: "Ford to City: Drop Dead"—and Howard Cosell droned, "The Bronx is burning," with cameras lingering on an enflamed school building during a Yankees game, could my six-year-old mind consider subway trains bombed with graf from top to bottom, front to back, anything other than the natural state of things?

HUNDREDS OF YOUNG BLACK TEENAGERS in the nosebleed uppermost rows of New York City's sold-out Madison Square Garden have tucked away gold necklaces inside their shirt collars. Bands of delinquent hiphop fans are snatching chains from the necks of the unsuspecting. Four friends seated nearby discuss similar incidents of thievery at last year's Fresh Festival, the only traveling hiphop concert tour we are aware of. My own fourteen-karat herringbone is a Christmas gift from two days ago. A brief mental reassessment passes; I unhook the chain and slip it into the pocket of my black-and-white checkerboard lumberjack coat. Before the end of the evening, five concertgoers are rushed to surgery at St. Vincent's Hospital; two are critically wounded by gunshots inside of the venue and three others are stabbed.

The headlining act has cancelled yet the Garden is no less crowded. Thousands of teens and twenty-somethings have braved a snowstorm for the Krush Groove Christmas Party. A one-shot extension of the fall's popular hiphop movie *Krush Groove*—the barely concealed life and times of Def Jam Records cofounder Russell Simmons—the show promised the most popular group in hiphop circa 1985: Run-D.M.C. Yesterday, Joseph "Run" Simmons (Russell Simmons's younger brother) suffered a pulmonary atelectasis. His left lung collapsed. Everyone expects the other reigning hiphop acts on the bill to perform all the more vigorously in compensation.

Accordingly, dapper MCs Dr. Jeckyll and Mr. Hyde take the stage in suits rhyming "The Champagne of Rap." Raising the level of spectacle, rap trio Whodini (wearing leather) roll onstage riding motorcycles to an ecstatically rapt audience. Their hit records—"Five Minutes of Funk," "Friends," "Funky Beat"—are followed word for word by my posse in the rafters. Then the sequined show girls appear, flanking a tuxedoed Kurtis Blow for "If I Ruled the World." He holds the Garden crowd transfixed through tunes like "Basketball" and "The Breaks" before roadies erect the façade of a mammoth radio. The tape cassette carriage ejects out seventeen-year-old LL Cool J, the de facto star of the show given Run's medical condition. "My radio, believe me, I like it loud! I'm the man with the box that can move the crowd!" he roars, shirtless in his trademark Kangol cap as hype man E Love bops beside him. LL Cool J continues: "I Can't Live Without My Radio" into "Rock the Bells" into "I Need a Beat." And then the surprise.

An unscheduled appearance by Doug E. Fresh and Slick Rick raises the energy level even higher. "The Show" ruled the handball courts of my neighborhood the entire summer—as well as the citywide rap-mix radio shows of DJs Red Alert and Chuck Chillout, and nightclubs my friends and I are all too young to attend—and they swiftly launch into the song. But this is not the surprise. The surprise is Mr. Bell—the forty-five-year-old music-appreciation teacher and choir director of my high school—onstage at my first concert ever, dressed as Inspector Gadget in a trenchcoat, black Ray-Bans and all, playing synthesizer on the hottest hiphop song of the year. My homeboys refuse to believe me.

"BELL AND I ARE COOL NOW," reads an entry from my journal years later—October 5, 1987. "I remember the first time I encountered (I won't say 'met') him. I was with Ronald, this overweight Jehovah's Witness Prince fan who left home because of differences with his mother. Ronald and I were in Bell's classroom. I picked up Bell's copy of Grandmaster Flash's 'Larry's Dance Theme.' He got pissed and I thought him conceited." Dennis Bell is listed along with Ollie Cotton as producer of "The Show" by Doug E. Fresh and the Get Fresh Crew. He is also coproducer of that group's 1986 debut album, *Oh, My God!,* and acted as their manager during the mid-1980s. This is the same period he taught at Truman High, currently listed as having the most reported felony incidents of all Bronx public high schools. As a sophomore I cut a few classes to play the Yamaha DX-7 keyboard in his classroom and soon signed up for his recording studio class to satisfy my music requirement.

When I was a junior, Dennis Bell selected me as the first of my classmates to meet him at Secret Sound Studios in downtown Manhattan to observe a recording session. I was sixteen marking equalizer levels with masking tape for a rap duo dubbed Nasty Cousins and pitching in party vocals for the backing track to "Brand New Funk," a song destined never to see the light of day. As a senior I drove down to a Chelsea restaurant named 20/20 early in the morning with my close friend Jay, one of my cronies from the Krush Groove concert, at the behest of Dennis Bell for a video casting. The director eventually chose me and several other classmates as dancing extras for Doug E. Fresh's "Keep Risin' to the Top" clip. (Was it my acid-wash shirt? My flattop haircut?)

At the head of my final school year, director Phil Joanou filmed the cream of Truman High's choir rehearsing "I Still Haven't Found What I'm Looking For" at Greater Calvary

Baptist Church in Harlem for a documentary about human-itarian rock band U2. That rehearsal, and my high school choir's subsequent Madison Square Garden performance backing U2 as the New Voices of Freedom, is a centerpiece scene of *Rattle and Hum*. Credits in the millions-selling soundtrack denote Dennis Bell as the musical director of that September 28, 1987 live performance. Much of this mise en scène—recording studios, music video shoots—presaged surroundings I would later become accustomed to as a music journalist. But my wonder years spent at a certain time (the golden age of hiphop) in a certain place (hiphop's gestation point) guaranteed that I would be only a few scant degrees of separation away from certain seminal figures, fur-ther cementing my visceral connection to the culture.

AYN RAND'S DESCRIPTION of the Howard Roark–designed Cortlandt Homes in *The Fountainhead* sounds a lot like Co-op City:

> The drawings of Cortlandt Homes presented six buildings, fifteen stories high, each made in the shape of an irregular star with arms extending from a central shaft. The shafts contained elevators, stairways, heating systems and all the utilities. The apartments radiated from the center in the form of extended triangles. The space between the arms allowed light and air from three sides. The ceilings were pre-cast; the inner walls were of plastic tile that required no painting or plastering; all pipes and wires were laid out in metal ducts at the edge of the floors, to be opened and replaced, when necessary, without costly demolition; the kitchens and bathrooms were prefabricated as complete units; the inner partitions were of light metal that could be folded into the walls to provide one large room or pulled out to divide it; there were few halls or lobbies to clean, a mini-

mum of cost and labor required for the maintenance of the place. The entire plan was a composition in triangles. The buildings, of poured concrete, were a complex modeling of simple structural features; there was no ornament; none was needed; the shapes had the beauty of sculpture.

Rand's is an approximate account of the buildings I grew up in from 1974 to 1993, on the twenty-seventh floor of one thirty-three-story building at 120 Elgar Place, then another at 140 Alcott Place. These are known as tower buildings, the tallest structures in Co-op City. The thirty-five buildings spanning the area—comprising 15,372 apartment units—are made up of these towers as well as chevron buildings twenty-four stories high and triple-core buildings that reach up to twenty-six flights. What is it like to come from a place like Co-op City? If I could make you understand that, I could make you understand the Bronx and perhaps nascent hiphop culture besides, for Co-op City *is* the Bronx, and the Bronx is proof that adversity and desperation are the seeds and fertile soil of invention; a locale where the oppositional coexistence of multiculturalism and white flight reiterated a familiar, inherently American allegory while simultaneously flipping the script.

In 1968 ground was broken for the construction of Co-op City in the northeast Bronx, reclaimed marshland alternately used during the sixties as a cucumber farm, a pickle factory, and an historical amusement park called Freedomland. Built by virtue of the Mitchell-Lama bill of New York State (passed to stifle New York City residents' exodus to the suburbs years before all the arson fires and omnipresent graf by Fuzz One, Phase 2, Kel 139, Noc 167, etc.), the complex is the largest apartment development in the United States, the largest cooperative apartment community in the world. The residents are technically shareholders of the Riverbay

Corporation that manages Co-op City as a Mitchell-Lama cooperative, electing fellow tenants to the Riverbay board of directors. Another truth of the area: Co-op City is a government-subsidized, middle-income housing project, also America's largest, with all that entails.

"Can anyone tell me why someone would invest $13,000 into a three-bedroom in Co-op and decide to move?" someone asks on an unofficial website devoted to the region. "It is not worth the investment." To which the webmaster—a former Co-op City resident—responds: "I don't know why someone would invest the equity either. In 1967, $4,000 was a good deal for my parents, compared to buying a home in Dix Hills, and they didn't think to live in the suburbs. I put $15k down and bought a six-room house on one-third-acre ten miles north of Boston four years ago—and I think it's appreciated $40k since then."

An anonymous contributor to the site offering a true Co-op City voice offers: "We were the original tenants of our unit. It was fun being one of the first families there as the place was being built. Some juvenile delinquents were in the complex, but probably not too bad by Bronx standards. It was neat to go up to the roof. On a clear day you could see clear across the Bronx to the Palisades. On windy days, the building swayed enough that in our 30th floor unit, you could see the water in the toilet swish back and forth. I liked the solid concrete construction and the central heat and A/C."

Ceil Stopler shares idyllic memories: "I lived in Co-op from 1969–1999, in building 4B. My three children were raised there and we can say we had the best times. When we first moved in from the Grand Concourse we thought we were living in luxury. Co-op City had many fine qualities and suburban living. It was where many people of ethnic backgrounds got together in harmony. The buildings were brand new and we thought it was paradise."

Historically, the Bronx famously held a sizable Jewish population; many moved to Pelham Parkway, Riverdale, and Co-op City as the rest of the borough began to degenerate. (I grew up in walking distance of the Traditional Synagogue of Co-op City: Young Israel of Baychester.) Many nationalities were indeed represented at the local schools I attended—classmates named Shiho Kawanishi, Joseph Weinholtz, Srinivas Vatti, Jasmine Peña, Sang Sook Pak, Manuel Fargas (his mother was my babysitter; his uncle, actor Antonio Fargas, portrayed Huggy Bear on television's *Starsky & Hutch* and starred in the cult film *Putney Swope*).

Eusebia Paez says, "The diverse ethnic backgrounds is wonderful to be in the middle of. My children have learned so much from so many kind neighbors. My youngest Andrew has been going to P.S. 153 where he has been exposed to so many different cultures that one month he decided that he was Mexican. Another month he was Jewish and still another he is African American culminating at this time with being Puerto Rican! We encourage his 'exploring' and respecting of all races while still remembering his roots. This couldn't be done in the communities that I grew up in."

The harmony of the situation is questionable. Another anonymous voice, quite possibly someone I attended school with, remarks: "I am one of the first few residents of Co-op City who is still left around. I was born in Co-op in 1970 and grew up around all u guys with older relatives who also lived here. As everyone has moved on I am still here watching the change take over. Believe me when I tell u what a sad story it is. One time ago u could go to the greenway and enjoy a night with ur friends on the stage laughing playing a couple of games. Well today if u care to do that u better have ur uzzi ready. I remember when Bartow use to have the mens store K.J. Look. I use to work there and Dreiser had the woman's store where u could get nice under clothing. Well now it is a card shop owned by nothing but the Indians. Oh and lets not forget the shoe repair in the Dreiser mall owned now by Russians. But the memory which really is gone from this all is the menorahs during Huankauk burning in the windows singing the songs that are sung at the services. Well now we live in a world of Kwanzaa who ever came up with that idea. Gee do wish Co-op City was still what it was years ago. Must soon invest in a bullet proff vest. So for those who are still here good luck stay off the drugs and those who have moved on u got out in the right time."

To which Miriam Rodriguez-Campbell responds: "These newcomers are what keep the community 'diverse.' But it seem that this word is not a part of your vocabulary. In case you haven't realized, this is America and all are welcomed. It seems as if you think Co-op City was built for only the Jews. Well, newsflash . . . it was built for everyone and if you no longer like it, MOVE!!! Keep in mind that Co-op City is a better place to live for many of its residents who previously lived under worse conditions. Those with negative attitudes only contribute to the rumors of this being a community going down the drain."

Surfing the site eventually uncovers some people I knew, though none of the black folks I remember. My lifelong classmate (from elementary to high school) Dara Bookman writes twice. Her first entry: "Co-op City was a great place for me to grow up in and I have great memories. The playground, paddleball courts, and the [Mister Softee] ice cream truck. I went to dance school there and met my best friend Veronica whom I am still best friends with till this day." Her second entry: "If Veronica Vitarius sees this contact me like right away. I miss you."

"So many people I know did not have the childhood we had! Lots of fun going to the Baychester Deli and buying quarts of Old-E!" writes Tommy Howell. I do not actually know Tommy Howell, though I am intimately familiar with the Olde English malt liquor to which he refers. Many Truman High students, myself included, cut classes for brew runs to cop and consume the beer popularized by rapper D.M.C.

B. Kemi Salako, who rather ironically has his own site dedicated to Co-op City, writes: "I've had a lot of fun and fond memories but it's losing its luster. I agree with one of the people in your guestbook who commented that it's like living in a cellblock. I have felt very isolated many times over the years, and I don't think it's a very lively, community-type environment, unless you grew up here and went to school here, or you're a teen who likes to hang out in the streets, or a senior who likes to sit on park benches and talk to their fellow residents all day. I don't think graffiti, spit, urine, etc. are acceptable in a dwelling of any kind, and it's a reflection of who is moving in and how little they value the property of others." Salako refers to an earlier entry by Adele Daigger: "My feelings are very mixed about Co-op City. I just never liked the whole high-rise concept, Co-op City was just too big and you never really knew who lived in your building or not. I also hated the elevators, it was like living in a prison cell block."

Divided into five sections like the wards of Houston, Co-op City has generated its most drama from Section Five. The story goes that by the time blacks and Latinos became hip to the construction of Co-op City in the late sixties, apartment units were already assigned to future tenants throughout the area and all the remaining apartments were in Section Five, which is physically isolated from the rest of the complex by a roadway known as Killer Curve. When a rivalry began between teens in Co-op City and others living across the New England Thruway (an area known as the Valley despite any apparent geological depression), animosity toward the Co-op kids concentrated on Section Five where I was raised. (My P.S. 160 classmate John Reed a/k/a Justice Allah nicknamed Section Five "the Power Section" in the 1980s.)

Gary Gonzalez, a former Truman High School acquaintance, sat trading college stories at two-thirty A.M. with four friends on benches in the back of his building at Hunter Avenue on June 7, 1992, when a roving crew of fifteen to twenty from the Valley approached. Nineteen-year-old Gonzalez spoke of transferring from the New York Institute of Technology to the City College of New York and switching his major to architecture as the thick posse fired gunshots outside a nearby Red Lobster, and again at a passing bus entering Killer Curve. Listening to his homeboy Joe Resto compare living in New Jersey with his former residence in Section Five, Gary Gonzalez was suddenly shot in the head by a bullet that ripped harmlessly through the shirt of another friend. The bullet that entered Resto "was in a sensitive area and could not be removed" at Jacobi Medical Center, according to the local *Co-op City Times*. Detective George Wood of the Forty-fifth Precinct determined the incident was a "senseless, random shooting—no words were exchanged." I remember Gary Gonzalez as a pretty boy whose attention from females sparked envy in his peers, the very picture of the kid who "never did nothing to nobody." I remember him as pitcher, shortstop, and co-captain of the Mustangs high school baseball team; in fact, he shared the number seven with Leonard Nelson, another tragically killed classmate, crushed to death on December 28, 1991 in a stampede at the infamous City College celebrity basketball game in which Sean Combs and rapper Heavy D were held partially responsible by Judge Louis Benza for the deaths of nine and the injuries of twenty-nine. Certainly Gary Gonzalez, as innocent in his own way as baby Kharel Slade, did not deserve to die. My homeboy from high school was guilty only of a childhood in Co-op City.

ONE SUMMER 2002 DAY I drive with my father through the South Bronx: to Findlay Avenue, Marcy Place, Cauldwell Avenue, St. Anns Avenue, and various Memory Lanes in-between. For all its reputation as a concrete jungle, more parks flourish in the Bronx than in any other borough, summer picnics galore in Van Cortlandt Park, Pelham Bay Park. Following One Hundred Seventieth Street into Claremont Avenue leads us by Claremont Park; the bountiful boughs of trees resurrect my memories of whiling away bucolic summers on metal swings and wooden seesaws. Dad's memory of Claremont Park is different. "You see those steps there?" he asks. "There would be times when there would be people—this is not an exaggeration—a hundred to a hundred-fifty people waiting for the drugs to come out. They'd be the whole length of the steps. The police would ride by and they wouldn't even say, 'Why are you standing here?' That's how out of control the Bronx was. They'd say, 'We can't sell over here 'cause the police are watching.' And the whole hundred people would move over *here*. Like, what, if they're watching, they're not seeing a hundred people leave?" We both laugh at the thought. "I used to think it was so stupid. The police were so actively involved in what was going on. Their thing was, if we wanted to kill ourselves, why should they stop us?"

My father and I cruise by 1520 Sedgwick Avenue, the eighteen-story building where hiphop began. Native Jamaican Clive Campbell a/k/a Kool DJ Herc—one third of the holy trinity of the inner-city fundamentalism of hiphop, alongside DJs Afrika Bambaataa and Grandmaster Flash—launched a cultural revolution throughout the South Bronx beginning with an innocuous birthday party for his sister Cindy in 1973. That gathering in the community center of this building right off the Major Deegan Expressway marked Kool Herc's first deejaying gig. My cousin Bea was the building manager of property on Sedgwick Avenue during the seventies, Dad says, perhaps even this building. Kool Herc's popularity induced him to branch out, spinning records at the Police Athletic League and eventually Bronx clubs like the Hevalo, the Twilight Zone, and the T-Connection.

Former Black Spades warlord Afrika Bambaataa, inspired in part by Kool Herc's deejaying, began performing at the Bronx River Community Center and soon formed the Zulu Nation, an organization of members encapsulating hiphop's four primary elements: deejaying, emceeing, breaking, and aerosol art. Elevating the existing DJ style of playing records, Joseph Saddler a/k/a Grandmaster Flash perfected mixing breakbeats—the most danceable, frenetic few seconds of any given song—at Bronx schoolyards and clubs like the Black Door and the Executive Playhouse. By assembling like-minded masses of DJs, rhymers, B-boys, graf artists, and general Bronx party people, this troika of pioneers produced the youth culture that nowadays makes millions for varied lifestyle and entertainment businesses across the globe.

Careening onto the Grand Concourse reminds me of the broad, elegant, tree-lined boulevard of Champs-Élysées in Paris; sure enough, later research confirms that French thoroughfare as the Grand Concourse's model. Still spinning tales of the Bronx, Dad relates the story of Adam Abdul Hakeem p/k/a Larry Davis. Recruited into a drug-selling ring of the Forty-fourth Precinct (the notoriously nicknamed Fort Apache) at the age of fourteen, Davis decided five years later to quit, inform the Federal Bureau of Investigation about the shady precinct, and go into hiding. In November 1986, twenty to thirty officers converged on the Bronx apartment of his sister to arrest him—or, as some claim, to assassinate him. "I'm talking ten, fifteen years ago when this neighborhood was out of control," Dad says. "What had happened was, he knew they were after him. He didn't go home. He was at his sister's house. When they came to his sister's house he had so many loaded weapons he shot his way out. They didn't hit him but *he* hit *them*." Larry Davis wounded six police officers single-handedly then escaped through an open window. "So then they had a 'shoot, kill him on sight' thing. And he sort of went to Gil Noble from *Like It Is* and C. Vernon Mason, and said, like, 'Get me to the police alive and I have a story for you.' So back then *Like It Is* was covering it with frequency." Authorities nevertheless arrested Larry Davis and sentenced him to five-to-fifteen years for the possession of weapons that the police allegedly provided him with when he was dealing drugs under their supervision.

We drive in silence then, over the Macombs Dam Bridge and out of the Bronx. I reminisce through all my lifelong accumulated mental snapshots of the Bronx, on what the borough was like during hiphop's infancy (my infancy) and hiphop's golden-age wonder years (my wonder years), before the culture was co-opted by capitalism, sidelining all hiphop elements less profitable than emceeing, before record companies expected every rap record to appeal to several million consumers worldwide. I reflect on that bygone era and reach the inevitable question: Is it what some are beginning to call the death of hiphop that I mourn, or my own childhood's end, the fleeting remembrance of things past?

FAMOUS NEGRO WRITER #77

WRITING ABOUT WRITING is as difficult for me as discussing my first love in intimate detail, so much so that I'm forcing myself to clear these first few paragraphs in haste, stream-of-consciousness style; please forgive the speed bumps. I first wrote because I read. Stories of the costumed adventurers who populate comics dominated my imagination starting at the age of three, and the preadolescent pastime of my friends and I creating our own superhero characters culminated in my first short story at fourteen: "I Was a Teenage Wolverine." Sports never appealed to me much growing up because I failed to understand why I should vicariously direct so much of my attention to the athletic talents of others, especially since dunking like Dr. J was something I'd never be capable of myself. Stan Lee, on the other hand, seemed to have little on me. Attending comic conventions in Manhattan hotel conference halls as a youth, meeting writers and artists on question-and-answer panels, the phenomenon of creation felt well within my grasp. These heroic stories with their cosmic grandeur fell flat for me without the proper illustrators involved, but I was fully aware of whose imagination stood behind these colorful adventures: writers. Science fiction held the celestial scope I was accustomed to, so Arthur C.

Clarke and Isaac Asimov novels were among the first additions to my personal library, along with the detective stories of Sir Arthur Conan Doyle's *The Collected Sherlock Holmes*. That I would ever be able to tackle someone with the fury of Mean Joe Greene was unlikely, but breaking the fourth wall of comics seemed easy—*Captain America* published my fan letter at eleven, and two more followed.

James Baldwin once said that you don't decide to be an artist, you discover that you are one, and that discovery took place for me as a teenager. Practicing artists surrounded me on all sides. My friend Jay hauled slabs of cardboard outside from underneath his bed to backspin on; I later tagged along with him and his Crazy Ass Bombers graf crew, spray-painting art throw-ups. My classmate Rahsean's rhymes, among those of other homeboys, rivaled flows of MCs on late-night radio. At fifteen I began writing poetry, though at that point I considered them song lyrics. (I took enough piano lessons as an eight-year-old to decipher sheet music and I practiced Prince tunes on the upright Kemble piano in my bedroom—a slightly atonal donation from my grandmother—with the leisure time my peers spent playing basketball, deejaying, and emceeing.) The celebrity voyeurism in my father's *Rolling Stone* magazines served as a guide to navigating life as an artist. I took honors English classes for granted; reading and writing were strong suits mainly because I'd always read and wrote. I presumed from early on that I would one day amass some creative body of work even if my Paisley Park contract didn't come through. Beginning the first of many journals at fifteen I fed my love for writing by writing.

James Baldwin went on to say that once you discover you are a writer, you haven't got any choice—you live that life or you won't live any. At twenty-four I returned in December 1995 from a fall semester of international law classes in

England with a slew of C- grades and a manuscript. Written abroad in three months, *Four Days in February* was a fictionalized account of my first major unrequited love experience, a coming-of-age story spanning three countries with a romantic triangle and heavy hiphop undertones. *Go Tell It on the Mountain* it was not, but during those late nights of cigarettes, Coke, chamomile tea, and breaking dawn picking at the scabs of freshly healed heartbreak, I came to the truth of Baldwin's pronouncement. Whether or not the book would ever be published, law school went out the window for me with "The End."

Mere months earlier I had become a contributing writer at *The Source* magazine—then the primary organ of hiphop culture, music, and politics. By college I had begun consuming magazines devoted to pop culture like the comics of my childhood, and long before my byline graced a glossy magazine I discerned the true service they provided. Editors seemed to stick their fingers in the air forecasting the upcoming developments in popular art (blockbuster movies, multiplatinum albums) and reporting those predictions to readers hungry for that sort of information; trend-spotting to aid subscribers in their conspicuous consumption, with the further assistance of advertisers pitching products in sync with the lifestyle aspirations the magazines promoted. By graduation I had immersed myself in enough of these glossies to naïvely entertain launching one. *Rolling Stone* ran consecutive cover stories on Michael Jackson, Jimi Hendrix, and Public Enemy (whose photo was replaced by an illustration for Hunter S. Thompson's "Fear and Loathing in Elko") my senior year, in January 1992. What if, I considered, every month was black month at *Rolling Stone,* if indeed there was a magazine totally devoted to black pop art with serious reportage, high-quality photography, all that? The premiere issue of

Vibe appeared eight months later, and recognizing that, I knew immediately I would work there. Seven years later, after writing record reviews in *Rolling Stone* for years, I would become a *Vibe* editor.

I then began to recognize the emergence of the Brooklyn Renaissance. A grouping of young black writers published in hiphop journals (*The Source, XXL, Vibe*) and arts weeklies (*The Village Voice, L.A. Weekly*) throughout the nineties would eventually end up producing books reflective of hiphop culture on some level or other. S. H. Fernando Jr. Lisa Jones. Bönz Malone. Elliott Wilson. Colson Whitehead. Veronica Chambers. Donnell Alexander. Hilton Als. Michael A. Gonzales. Karen R. Good. Jefferson Mao. Touré. Havelock Nelson. Sacha Jenkins. Danyel Smith. Ronin Ro. Kenji Jasper. Selwyn Seyfu Hinds. Frank Williams. Kevin Powell. Smokey D. Fontaine. Robert Marriott. Asha Bandele. Bakari Kitwana. Ayana D. Byrd. kris ex. Joan Morgan. Gabriel Alvarez. Kandia Crazy Horse. Cheo Hodari Coker. dream hampton. The vast majority of these writers rested their heads at some point in the Clinton Hill, Fort Greene, Park Slope, or Bedford-Stuyvesant sections of Brooklyn. The inevitability of the hiphop literati movement was clear as day to me.

In my romantic ruminations I grew excited to be swept up in a movement that might make the cultural, historical impact of the 1920s Harlem Renaissance, the thirties Negritude movement of Paris, or the sixties Black Arts movement. The Algonquin round table of the twenties and thirties likewise came to mind, writers associated with the *New Yorker* and *Vanity Fair* trading barbed witticisms over mixed drinks in midtown Manhattan's Algonquin Hotel. The Beats of the 1950s smoked joints, preoccupied themselves with bebop, and created some enduring literature. Going through the same motions as writers of these arts collectives from the past, I expected greatness from what some of us derisively deemed the hiphop niggarati.

I grew up fast, yet in some ways perhaps not fast enough. After interning at *Vibe* at twenty-two, working on the first issues that would establish the publication as an official ongoing monthly, I paid dues writing gratis for now-defunct titles like *Noir* and *Freedom Rag* while enrolled at Fordham Law School. *The Source* experienced an infamous editorial walkout in November 1994 and, strapped for writers, senior editor Adario Strange soon telephoned with some assignments. *True*—a British, highbrow urban glossy which later became the fashion magazine *Trace*—launched during the 1995 summer that my byline in *The Source* first appeared; editor/publisher Claude Grunitzky showed me around London and assigned some work when I studied abroad later that year. When I returned having penned *Four Days in February,* the fact that I'd attempted a novel impressed editors into proffering more thought pieces, album reviews, and celebrity profiles in 1996. By that fall I'd found my own garden apartment in Clinton Hill, two blocks away from 226 St. James Place, where the Notorious B.I.G. was raised.

By that winter, *Rolling Stone* solicited my opinion on the debut album of Erykah Badu. Months later I took a job with a teenage fanzine to ensure my rent was paid as my body of work was building. *Rap Pages* executive editor Allen S. Gordon offered to serialize excerpts of *Four Days in February,* which ran over three issues in 1998. *XXL* editor-in-chief Sheena Lester hired me as deputy editor that summer, the very month *The Source* published my first cover story: reporting the breakup of hiphop's seminal A Tribe Called Quest. A year later, *Vibe* top editor Danyel Smith lured me with over double my *XXL* salary and there I was, installed as music editor in the office I'd coveted in my Morehouse senior year. (And, in fact, these various editorial posts were not terribly far removed from the fictional positions held by the *Daily Planet*'s Clark Kent or the *Daily Bugle*'s Peter Parker that I'd read of as a youngster.) (And did you know that comics come from the Bronx? They're the 1934 invention of Max Gaines, a salesman from the borough.)

I could say disillusion over my Brooklyn Renaissance concept set in at this point, but disillusionment isn't as accurate a descriptor as maybe maturity. I discovered early on that friendship is not necessarily sparked or maintained on the basis of a common association in the hiphop literati. In my earlier days as an aspiring music journalist, I imagined more of a one-big-happy-family atmosphere; situations are always perceived differently from the outside. This notion was not totally dashed. Author Karen R. Good hosted some memorable house parties; I smoked some choice buds with kris ex listening to Wu-Tang Clan advance music and watching a bootleg of director Hype Williams's *Belly*; one of the most treasured romances of my twenties centered on former *Honey* magazine editor-in-chief Asondra R. Hunter; on and on. But writers are notorious for the web of egocentricity, insecurities, neuroses, and jealousies that dominates our psyches, often fuels our art, and drives our mates up the wall—and eventually these factors beset many of our relationships. These are people, not bylines made flesh. You will like some and you will dislike others; don't think Dorothy Parker didn't make enemies.

Another loose peg in my Brooklyn Renaissance construction was the work itself. Writers rather conceitedly sized themselves up against Ralph Ellison on the basis of, say, reviewing an Ice Cube record. Ralph Ellison produced some solid jazz criticism in his day but he also authored *Invisible Man,* one of the most celebrated works of the twentieth century. Consorting with celebrities on a semi-regular basis can encourage an exaggerated sense of one's own importance. I should have anticipated the swelled heads and rarefied airs put on by young black writers, but even more dismaying, the haute attitudes were disproportional to the work. I hoped our legacy lay with Langston Hughes, not Lester Bangs. (Time will tell.)

I also ultimately had to face the reality that a hiphop literati movement could never possess the gravitas of movements past because literature no longer holds the same space in society. The Internet, DVD collections, shortened MTV attention spans, and hundreds of cable television channels have all contributed to transforming America into a less literate nation. Mediocrity currently reigns on bestseller lists, and work aspiring to the level of *Their Eyes Were Watching God* and *The Fire Next Time* of old is left on the shelf for escapist, entertaining easy reading. Which is to say that the opportunities for reaching a mass audience have perhaps fled to cinema, but the dilemma of mediocrity persists even there. Not that a hiphop literati movement of essayists, poets, playwrights, and fiction writers isn't in full swing despite this intellectually vapid environment, but it took some personal readjustment to conceive the realities of this postmillennial arts renaissance. That reassessment also led to some reevaluation of why I write.

At the time that my membership in the hiphop literati began feeling like a booby prize, *The Village Voice* asked me to review a global anthology of writers from the African diaspora. The book was edited by _____ _____, one of the writers I interned for at *Vibe*, drove to Philadelphia with for a Lollapalooza concert in the early nineties, and solicited advice from during those days. When I had initially learned of the book I submitted a short story to _____ _____ but had missed the deadline. That he had not extended an invitation for my involvement to begin with suggested to me that the hiphop literati had little sense of solidarity (a notion exacerbated by my then-recent dismissal from *Vibe* when the fashion editorial director succeeded to editor-in-chief) and that this was not a writer whom I was too close with to critique for *The Village Voice*. Besides, I would not be reviewing the work of _____ _____ himself because the book was an anthology of other writers. I accepted the assignment; I didn't feel our previous interactions posed an objectivity issue. I read the book and enjoyed it, filing a piece including praise like, "[The book] does an effective job documenting these disparate voices," and, "The critical essays in this new volume are the high point," proceeding to extol the work of four essayists.

My main critical assessment, not surprisingly, stemmed from _____ _____'s introduction wherein he championed a new movement in literature. "For the prototypal hiphop journalist—somewhere between his badge-wearing embrace of that identity and his fierce, discomfiting disdain of same—the romantic, highfalutin hope is to go down in history as a seminal writer in a similar collective," I wrote. "The work should come first, and following its influential reverberations, the espying and espousal of movements should follow." Months after the review ran in 2001 an elbow bumped me, as I was walking along Eighth Street in Greenwich Village with bags in hand. I stopped and brief seconds passed before my mind registered _____ _____ standing before me with a lady friend.

"What's up, man?" I asked, transferring both bags to one hand and offering a handshake. I was left hanging.

"Take your glasses off," he gruffly commanded. _____ _____ wanted eye contact. I removed my sunglasses and set my bags on the ground.

"Wow, we have beef again?" I asked. We'd gone through a

patch eight years prior over another minor perceived slight, and actually, _____ _____ held a reputation for being disagreeable, falling out publicly with others in the hiphop community. My turn had come around again.

"Ain't no 'wow.' You challenging my knowledge of hiphop?" he asked. "That review was shady. All you talked about was hiphop journalism. You're just mad because you're not in the book. Don't ever write about me ever again!"

He motioned closer, shouting now. Passersby began to stare.

"I can tell you didn't even read the whole book. And your review was mad personal. What does your birthday party have to do with it? You're just mad because I didn't come to your birthday party."

I made the point in my review, per *The Village Voice*'s personalizing style, that I knew nine of the anthology's hundred-plus writers, but my objectivity was untainted because none of the nine were close enough friends to attend my recent thirtieth birthday party. I attempted to deflate the article's personalized tone by dividing it into three sections self-deprecatingly titled "pithy navel-gazing insights." My editor and I thought it was funny.

"Wow. I'm not challenging you," I said, trying to remain calm. "I respect your knowledge of hiphop. The review wasn't all about hiphop journalism. I mentioned fiction by Christopher John Farley and . . ." I paused to notice bystanders reacting to the scene _____ _____ was creating in broad daylight.

"Yo, you're gonna have to step back," I said. His face was inches from mine, like a schoolyard challenge. My last fistfight was in the twelfth grade. I began to push him backwards.

"Don't touch me!" he shouted angrily.

"This isn't worth it," his female companion told him,

intervening. "Your review was mad personal," she reiterated to me. _____ _____ backed off.

"You're a herb writer," he said. "I would never let somebody step to me on the street like this. I'll forgive you this time. Forgive, but never forget."

_____ _____ smiled at me like the proverbial Cheshire cat, seething. I lifted my bags to leave. I was prepared to debate the points of my review but it became clear he only wanted to vent and possibly provoke me into scrapping. I started stepping.

"Write about this!" he yelled as I walked away, his homegirl holding him back by this point in that familiar playground fashion. "We're watching you. We know where you're at: 52 Cambridge Place!"

I turned back briefly upon hearing my Brooklyn address _____ _____ had memorized. "You're on my dick," I mumbled to myself. _____ _____ spat in my direction, missing. I crossed Eighth Street to Electric Lady Studios and kept walking.

On a hiphop conference panel a year later I recounted this episode before an assembled audience. The panel was about karma. Shortly after our altercation, police arrested _____ _____ for destroying the eyeglasses of writer Knox Robinson at a Brooklyn street festival over a perceived disrespect. I told the listeners that the law of karma involves cause and effect, and by _____ _____ believing that I needed to be punished for trashing his anthology (cause), a punishment was exacted upon him for attacking Knox Robinson (effect). After our confrontation I called my father to laugh about it. After their confrontation Knox Robinson called the police department.

The weekend following the panel my telephone rang; it was _____ _____. He had been told about the panel discussion and wanted to have a reasoned conversation to put the conflict behind us. A half hour later we sat in my living room and resolved everything, calm and collected. Imamu Amiri Baraka once told me a story of visiting Ralph Ellison's Harlem home after critiquing his essay collection *Shadow and Act* and being chased down St. Nicholas Avenue by his Scottish terriers. James Baldwin alienated former mentor Richard Wright after debating the merits of the protest novel in an essay indicting *Native Son*. So, I don't know. Maybe there *is* a Brooklyn Renaissance. Come 2002 I moved to Harlem, next door to an apartment building where Paul Robeson once lived.

I am not a loyalist to any specific art form. I write because I believe I have some things to say. Initially I felt the need to join the ranks of artists that I've recognized my reflection in all my life; failing to do so might have had calamitous results, of the usual dream-deferred variety. With time I grew to determine my vision for society—a world of independent thinkers where people take a more spiritual perspective on life—and decided that the most effective way to help bring this about was to prophecy through creative arts, to live life and express these experiences for others to glean something from. Functional art can aid in healing mental and spiritual states, and the hiphop community and beyond are in need of both. Modern American society largely posits art as a medium for escapism and entertainment. However, the ancient aesthetic of African creativity holds that art should be utilitarian, that it serve some functional purpose.

"After I read this," Baraka once told me, "what am I supposed to do?" What action, in other words, is this literature telling me to take? I believe in a balance between entertaining art and a more purposeful approach with an underlying, subliminal agenda. *Think for yourself* and *Consider our divine source* are the main things I wish to get across, why I write as of today. Determining a hundred more ways of expounding on these themes is what I'd like to spend a few more decades of my artistic life doing.

THE SUCKERPUNCH OF MY CHILDHOOD FILES

M Y FATHER HAS THE POWER to cloud the minds of men. Like the Shadow, he says.

As a teenager I recurrently handed over test tubes of urine for my father to take back to his job, my piss swishing back and forth in his briefcase on the way to his Manhattan office. I cannot recall exactly why I did it—what reason Dad offered for needing those occasional bottles of pee. Whatever my doubts, I hit the bathroom when asked. He was my dad.

Faucets flowed overtime in my family's three-bedroom Bronx apartment over the years, the resonance of rushing water muffling the evidence of things not seen. One late night near two A.M. the front door opened and shut, the bathroom door closed, and the tub ran for nearly an hour. I needed to use the bathroom. I knocked, opened the door. His nostrils dusted with white powder, my father excused himself for my privacy. The following day, my heart beating nervously, I called his Manhattan office, telling Dad of a dream I had involving his emerging from the bathroom with cocaine on his nose. He couldn't imagine why I would have dreamed such a thing.

I steered my black Huffy Bandit through a six-story garage years prior, excitedly searching for my folks' brand-new 1980

Pontiac Sunbird. I slowly approached our two-day-old ride on the third floor with surprise; the car's front end was mangled. A combination of Quaaludes and alcohol had led to my father's accident the previous night. A welcoming committee later awaited Dad's return from his Manhattan office: his wife, his mother, his grandparents. He couldn't imagine how the car became dented. They put in a police report for a hit-and-run. My father was thirty. Seven years later our white Audi ended up crushed beyond repair, totaled in a similar accident.

The year of the Sunbird wreck I would visit Dad in rehab for the first time, on Manhattan's Upper East Side at Smithers Addiction Treatment Center. He worked as a telecommunications supervisor in the 1970s and 1980s (a position I failed to understand until my twenties), and at that point his employer, Metropolitan Life Insurance, paid for his twenty-eight-day detox and therapy. Smithers treated my father for alcoholism but he'd also been sniffing heroin regularly since his City College days, on breaks from the post office. Dad's program coerced me—a nine-year-old—to write some paragraphs about the impact of his actions on the family. I'm sure I compared him with Iron Man; Tony Stark had issues. The only time my mother, father, or I have ever trekked to the refined summertime seashore of East Hampton was for Dad's twenty-eight-day stay at the Seafield Center in 1986. Absent that Thanksgiving, he later checked out of a treatment program for cocaine and alcohol addiction on my sixteenth birthday, this second period courtesy of his bosses at Mobil Oil. My father used one drug or another over the course of thirty years, including crack. It was the death of the grandfather who raised him which finally drove Dad to Bronx Lebanon Hospital, then to a spiritually based treatment facility in Queens where he ultimately became drug-free at the age of forty-nine.

You are possibly none too curious about the personal foibles of my father, even in this age of confessional culture and reality-TV knee-jerk soul bearing. Walk with me for a while, though, and the stroll may reveal as much about the nature of hiphop as can be learned from the most gifted of MCs. If the late J.F.K. Jr. represents American royalty—a true American son as the Kennedy experience stands in for the American dream writ large—then I (perhaps not so) humbly submit myself as a prince of hiphop America. Born in the Bronx in 1970, present at ground zero of the emergent culture for all its subsequent stages, I feel this is no hyperbolic claim (even if I'm ego-tripping in true hiphop fashion). Dad's troubles are not laid out for my ghetto-pass credentials. On "Poppa Was a Playa," Nas relates the traumatic childhood experience of catching his father, jazz musician Olu Dara, snorting cocaine with a woman not his mother. Nas's antagonist Jay-Z, in "Moment of Clarity," shares the pain of growing up the fatherless son of a heroin abuser. Eminem has expressed that he's never met his father and has no interest in ever meeting him. That the childhoods of three of the most skilled and celebrated hiphop storytellers are riddled with paternal contention serves my argument—much of the male-posturing pathos of rap music stems from an identity struggle, the hypermasculine bluster of certain rhymes and images a result of manhood defined out of environs where fathers were absent, destructive, or sources of shame. The nihilistic violence, the disrespect toward females, and even self-hatred in hiphop cannot be properly grasped without an understanding of how the sins of the father often visit the son.

ON THAT NOTE, I began drinking alcohol at the age of fourteen as a freshman in high school. A small band of classmates and I ducked out of Truman High to a local bodega from time to time for forty-ounce bottles of malt liquor: Private

Stock, Ballantine Ale, Olde English, Night Train. This cannot be very much different from the experience of many American teenagers except for the foreknowledge of my father's detox programs.

As a cautionary example, my dad's challenges probably mitigated the most against my trying marijuana. I knew twelve-year-olds toking in the eighth grade but I wouldn't hit a bong until my sophomore year of college, with my roommate, his friends from Evanston, Illinois, and my old prom date visiting me in Atlanta. This was 1989, three years before *The Chronic* detonated hiphop and Dr. Dre madly popularized smoking weed. I can count the amount of times I puffed herb during those years on one hand. I was more apt to sip from small flasks of Jack Daniel's or Southern Comfort—aping rock guitarists like Slash and Keith Richards (we share the same birthday)—as my rowdier college cronies guzzled beer in search of weekend bacchanalia. My girlfriend and I smoked on I-85 with another couple on our way from Georgia to Panama City Beach, Florida, for spring break. We did it again that New Year's Eve at the Central Park West apartment of some girlfriend of hers. There was a night of bar-hopping that summer with the night-shift crew of Tower Video that led to some hits of a joint in my manager's backseat. Fraternity brothers clouded up my bathroom off-campus at a house party the following semester and I joined in. And right before graduation the visit of my best friend from the Bronx resulted in a TV night of Seal unplugged, stoned with an old high school homegirl and her roommate. Measure that up against an average undergrad student at Brown.

One of my closest friends smokes daily; hanging out in his Brooklyn apartment post-graduation I joined the hiphop zeitgeist, burning trees more often. Snoop Doggy Dogg was the most popular rap star of the moment; Cypress Hill had ties to the marijuana advocacy group NORML; Method

Man was blowing smoke on magazine covers. My by then ex-girlfriend taught me how to roll a blunt with a Phillies cigar the same summer night she introduced me to D'Angelo's *Brown Sugar*. (What a revoltin development.) I'd long lost sight of my father's cautionary example; slowly seeping into the ranks of the hiphop literati I was looking the gonzo spirit of Hunter S. Thompson straight in the eye. Fort Greene, Brooklyn, 1996, as I passed a White Owl to Erykah Badu in the back of my Chevy, my father was hawking stolen bits of bullshit to bodega cashiers for heroin cash, sleeping in the station wagon he'd stolen from my great-grandfather.

In my adolescence, Prince was a longtime hero—bucking moneymaking inclinations for creative growth taught me a great deal about the path of the artiste—and he always publicly frowned on drugs. But I had other heroes: Hendrix, Lennon, Morrison. Drug-experimenting heroes. Ergo, the day I dropped acid that summer was amazing. One of my best friends' roommates had tabs. That July day the annual Morehouse/Spelman alumni picnic raged on in Fort Greene Park. I stalked the grounds with my homeboy, tripping, a huge tree branch in hand as my staff. Whenever I think of that sunny afternoon I'm always drawn back to the dog with the Frisbee. I felt such an empathy with this German shepherd leaping for the Frisbee thrown by his owner, a glint in his eye as he caught the thing in his teeth; my heart swelled as if the dog was a friend who got something he really wanted or was trying to make me proud. The breeze blowing through tree leaves filtering beaming sun rays was incredible, the wave of energy detectable in the rippling foliage.

Cocaine I've snorted four or five times, with the *Brown Sugar* babe each time. The first, at her Brooklyn pad on Fulton Street, I mainly remember feeling like Superman (stop me if you've heard this before), like I could do anything—invigorating wind on my face, extremely talkative; I never felt the purported sexual rush. My final experiment with lines, in a bathroom at Lemon, ended with almost losing my wallet later at Spy Bar and rejecting sex with my ex, the last time she ever offered. This was 1998. Ecstasy has passed through my system four times to date. The first was the monster. My memory of an unconsummated high school crush and I dancing close and slow to Miles Davis's "Générique" will live forever—kissing, embracing. An ashtray full of Marlboro Lights butts. Ecstasy made us very chatty but also emotionally open. Another former flame and I sat through Woody Allen's *Celebrity* in a darkened Gramercy theater ingesting mushrooms. I had a powerful urge for cigarettes afterward, a strong impression from Leonardo DiCaprio. The high was similar to Ecstasy; the sentimental empathy, the Superman effect also.

Somewhere around the time I chose to make a living as a writer, I decided (discovered?) that part of my purpose is to refract life experiences through my own personal prism, as well as to champion independent thinking. Find out for yourself, I say. In the course of my own experiments in better living through chemistry, I've come to a few conclusions. First, you get what you expect. If you silence fear and seek mind expansion and meditation in drugs that alter your perceptions, then you're likely to find what you seek. If instead you turn to drugs for escape, to numb pain, to get blotto, you're likely to find that too, but only temporarily. Second, as critic Ann Powers explains in *Weird Like Us: My Bohemian America*, "Drugs offer an encounter with the random self, a step beyond the rational into aspects of one's physical and psychic being that can be named only when they surge forth. Taking drugs is like taking an airplane ride inside your own head; you can arrive safely or crash, and fastening your seat belt may or may not save you . . . It takes focus to do this well. Many people fail, spinning beyond the grasp of themselves, while others luck out and stay intact without even trying." Due to my lack of an addictive personality and/or my mother praying over my brothers and I as children, I thankfully count myself among the latter. My twenties—long self-described as my extended teenage years—slink further and further behind and I've by now learned whatever lessons drugs tempt to teach.

MY FATHER HAD NEVER KNOWN HIS BIOLOGICAL FATHER. His grandparents raised him on Amsterdam Avenue in Harlem while his mother worked as a supervisor at AT&T to support her family. Such was the way in the fifties and sixties. My father loved comics—I later weaned my reading skills on thousands left over in Great-grandma's closet—and later, he loved music. A Motown Revue concert in Forest Hills, Queens, ended in a chance meeting with Temptations valet Roosevelt "Bucky" Smith and Dad landed the enviable position of running errands and setting up equipment as a local roadie for the quintet's New York City shows from 1966 to 1969. New Year's Day 1970, my father brought in the seventies alone in an audience of thousands, serenaded by Jimi Hendrix playing "Auld Lang Syne" at the Fillmore East (a gig recorded as *Band of Gypsys*). Two months later he almost missed the surprise twentieth birthday party my mother had planned out, in lieu of a Miles Davis performance at the Fillmore East; they caught an earlier show instead (recorded as *Live at the Fillmore East: It's About That Time*). Nine months later Dad was a married man and I was born, named for both Miles Davis and James Marshall Hendrix. (A bootleg of my birth no doubt circulates somewhere, *Brenda's Got a Baby: M.M.L. Alive at the Sloane Hospital for Women*.) Yet my father never knew his own biological father . . . until the three of us had drinks in downtown Manhattan in 1991.

My great-grandfather Henry L. Johnson lived to be

eighty-five in a rent-controlled, three-bedroom South Bronx apartment. In one of the few lengthy conversations I held with him as a young adult, I managed to ask him about my father's father. Truth is, I have no recollection of Frank Lewis, the man whose family name I uphold, the man who adopted my father a few years after marrying my grandmother. They divorced before I was born. I was to learn from my parents at sixteen that my father had never personally known his biological dad, a man named Aaron Plummer. Great-grandpa Johnson seemed just the person to ask for details, as long as we happened to be straining for conversation over a fifty-seven-year generation gap. *This is what you can tell me,* I thought. *Who was Aaron Plummer?* Great-grandpa relayed our discussion to my grandmother as if all we spoke of was Aaron Plummer. Grandma checked an old phone number of a cousin of his who she infrequently corresponded with, and he was swiftly located in nearby Maplewood, New Jersey. Calls were placed. A photograph of Aaron Plummer with his wife soon arrived in the mail. More calls were placed. Shortly we scheduled drinks downtown with Dad's dad.

I drank a tequila sunrise, three actually, the only time I've ever shared drinks with my father. At the Globetrotter Restaurant (now gone) connected to the Hotel Penta (now the Hotel Pennsylvania) on Seventh Avenue, my father, Aaron Plummer (it happens everyone calls him Jacques), and I spoke for an hour. My newfound grandfather's family had migrated north from New Orleans; they were Creole. A chemical engineer with two adult children, he traveled the world on business and pleasure. And he loved jazz. I remember him paying for everything with a Diners Club card, and thinking, *They still make those?* Snapshots ensued. Days later, Dad met his half-sister, half-brother, and his father's wife at their home in New Jersey, a trip I thought he should make by himself. My father was forty-one. After meeting his father he would continue to abuse heroin for another eight years.

"In an increasingly dangerous and unpredictable world, absent fathers add tremendously to the insecurity of children."
—Haki R. Madhubuti

MAMA'S GUN

THERE WAS A ROUTINE to visiting my grandmother's house in the 1980s: greet Grandma; crack open a White Rose soda from the fridge (the first of several); run upstairs to the "Little Room" (my uncle Sheldon's old childhood room) to talk with Grandma a bit; then sit in front of the living room TV for hours and gorge on *Battle of the Planets, Gilligan's Island, Three's Company,* etc. Grandma would ask if I'm hungry. Maybe she'd cook some salmon cakes. One hour by two buses, a half-hour by foot, ten minutes by car from Co-op City—Two Hundred Thirty-third Street, near the Edenwald housing projects of Grandmixer D.XT and the Funky Four + One. By the time my bus rides were done, my Walkman would have finished playing an entire album—in the summer of 1986, maybe something like Sheila E.'s *Romance 1600.*

This day I bound into the Little Room, and laying on the ironing board was a vinyl copy of Salt-N-Pepa's *Hot Cool & Vicious.* (A caveat: my late grandmother—born Bessie Eva Greene—was pretty hip. She was fifty-six at the point of this tale. Of her four sisters and five brothers from the small, rural town of Clover, Virginia, she was the only sister to relocate to Harlem as a teenager in the forties, marrying numbers banker "Amsterdam" Earl Benton. She wore an Afro sometime in the seventies. She twice told her doting first-born grandson the story of how she happened to smoke weed with Billie Holiday in the 1940s, visiting a mutual friend up in Harlem. I once found a nickel bag in the pocket of my mom's coat, a coat she borrowed from my grandmother. So Grandma might actually have been checking for Salt-N-Pepa—one never knows—though her taste tended more toward Gladys Knight and Al Green. My grandpa sometimes called her "Kiddo.")

I laughed. "Grandma, what you know about Salt-N-Pepa?"

"Oh, Sheldon brought that by," she said, handing me the album. "That's your cousin Pam." Pamela Greene, DJ Spinderella of Salt-N-Pepa's first album, fell out with the group and was replaced by Deirdre Roper by the time "Push It" made the group a pop phenomenon in 1987. Cousin Pam and I have never met but she inadvertently blessed me with bragging rights for a year. And I dubbed *Hot Cool & Vicious* from my grandma.

This is for my cousin Pam, Sha-Rock, Angie B, Blondie, DJ Pambaataa, Debbie D, Lisa Lee, Little Lee, Sweet, Sour, DJ Wanda D, Lady B, Pebblee Poo, the Dynamic Dolls, Daisy Castro, Lady Pink, Lady Heart, Missy Dee, Dimples D, Roxanne Shanté, the Real Roxanne, Sparky D, E-Vette Money, Salt, Pepa, Spinderella, DJ Jazzy Joyce, MC Lyte, Queen Latifah, Sweet Tee, Antoinette, Ms. Melodie, Sistah Souljah, Nikki D, Yo Yo, Da Brat, Left Eye, the Lady of Rage, Lauryn Hill, Shorty No Mas, Bahamadia, Harmony, Heather B, Queen Pen, Missy Elliott, Mia X, Rah Digga, Lil' Kim, Amil, Foxy Brown, Charli Baltimore, Eve, Vita, Trina, Rokafella, Miss Jade, Ms. Dynamite, Jean Grae, Free, and more mother goddesses of hiphop.

Spiritualists of my generation criticize Christianity for smothering the feminine principle underneath a sheet in the

Holy Trinity ("The Father, the Son, and the Holy Ghost? What about the Mother?"). The same critique can be leveled against hiphop. The misogynistic bitch-and-ho parlance of the nineties tempered off somewhat during the aughts, replaced by rap videos with undulating backsides and the strip-club atmospherics of sweaty breasts and thighs. With its sportsmanship-competitive tone and patriarchal attitude, hiphop has never been too kind to its feminine principle, present (naturally) since the culture's very beginning. This book is a collection of autobiographical literary essays direct-ing attention in large part to the troubles of hiphop culture. One of those troubles is that hiphop needs balance: posi-tive/negative balance, old-school/next-school balance, femi-nine/masculine balance. In that interest—and in the spirit of 2Pac's "Dear Mama," De La Soul's "I Am I Be," and Ghostface's "All That I Got Is You"—I offer some reflections from the matriarchal side of my Bronx rearing.

WE CARAVANNED DOWN TO CLOVER annually when I was growing up. Grandma Benton had two brothers living in the Bronx and Harlem—my great-uncles Carl and Melvin—and we all (my parents included) raced down I-95 in August three or four cars deep to visit extended family in Virginia. The Bethel Grove Baptist Church held a homecoming Sunday service every summer and the Greene family made a weekend reunion out of it. Melvin Greene returned to live in Clover with his wife Jackie when I was a tweener, and his home became ground zero for all my cousins, great-aunts, -uncles, and in-laws from New York City and Baltimore. As part of a second-generation of African Americans to be raised in the North, I witnessed tighter bonds between up-North and down-South black families than generally exist now.

Barbeque chicken, grilled cheeseburgers, and the like were prepared out front of Uncle Melvin's, the gravel driveway lined with a half dozen cars. Cows grazing in a yard next door gazed curiously. Relatives warned my young cousins and I to beware of leeches as we explored through wooded areas. Races, make-believe, tag, hide-and-go-seek. It was fun to trap hornets inside Silly Putty egg containers, threatening my girl cousins with them. I couldn't move two steps without an annoying fly, mosquito, or gnat flying in my face, crawling up my skin. We played baseball games in the backyard, children and adults hitting fly balls over Uncle Melvin's ranch-style house.

Africa holds a mystique for black folks curious of their roots, but the South is a motherland with an easier trail to follow, and Mom's family gave me the only down-South experience I'd have as a youngster. As I have said, my father never knew his own father and his New Orleans–based family. His mother's parents, the Johnsons, were from Brunswick, Georgia, but Dad never had much fun visiting there as a child and didn't want to subject me to the place. Grandpa Benton was also from Georgia—the town of Baxley—but his relations all moved elsewhere, so I've never been. Grandpa Benton's sister Ada moved to the small town of Leesburg, Florida, where I spent some teenage summertime days when Grandpa bought a vacation home there.

(A note on my late grandfather: Aside from marrying a Southern girl, Earl Benton led a life worthy of his own memoirs. He joined the Army in the 1940s, lying about his age to leave rural Baxley behind. They ordained him a minister there, not because of his religious inclinations, but because he hit it off with his regiment's preacher. He ran numbers—a central element of Harlem social life for decades—on Amsterdam Avenue until his retirement, and was briefly jailed when I was still in diapers. Grandpa owned a laundromat and residential property in Harlem, selling one of his buildings to actress Clarice Taylor, Cliff Huxtable's mom on *The Cosby Show*. I placed bets on horses at Yonkers Raceway on family outings led by Grandpa; imagine racing forms and dream books on my grandparents' chest of drawers. I recall gambling trips to Atlantic City, swimming in the hotel pools. His cars, never over two years old, always had new-car smell. With his penchant for cigars and fedoras, Grandpa always somewhat reminded my mother of James Cagney in *White Heat*. Earl Benton was a man of his word, yet a man of few words. Whatever upper-middle-class and/or gangsta roots I might lay claim to come from Grandpa. My grandma often called him "Amsy," for Amsterdam Avenue.)

For two weeks one summer I vacationed with Grandma Benton in Virginia, bored to tears, annoying everyone around me. My great-grandmother Emma Greene stayed in Baltimore near some of her daughters for years, eventually living in a trailer home in Clover on the property of my aunt Mattie. There, I read through all my comic books in one day, guzzled tall-necked glass bottles of Coca-Cola, and impatiently counted off the days till our return to New York. The heat was oppressive, the thirteen-inch TV broadcast too much snow, and I asked Grandma about going home every hour on the hour. (She never lost her patience, though my mom wouldn't hear the end of it for a while.) As a nine-year-old city boy, laying back and giving in to the simpler pleasures of the South didn't occur to me. The value of spending quality time with my septuagenarian great-grandmother didn't register. (She was born in 1905. Her grandfather was Native American, my great-great-great-grandfather.) Fifteen years later, at the double wedding of my uncle Melvin's daughters, things were different. The echo of my late grandmother in the voices, features, and mannerisms of her remaining sisters and brothers was bittersweet—a comfort, yet saddening somehow. Drinking whiskey and puffing joints at a local jook joint shack with my now adult cousins was cool—dirt roads, fireflies, crickets, brighter stars, cleaner air. When Mom moved from the Bronx to a gated community near the Poconos years later, right off, the area reminded me of her girlhood Clover.

IN THE MID-NINETIES, permanently on my own for the first time, I found myself reading what I'd always considered to be my mother's type of books: spiritual self-improvement titles by James Redfield, M. Scott Peck, and others. As a teen I had derided new-age literature as hokey, casting a cynical eye on its readers as too dim to diagram their own self-development. But discussing spiritual insights with my mother now raised our relationship to a higher level; I became closer to Mom and my spirit simultaneously. While talking over her interests, I discovered depths to Mom's wisdom that I'd slept on before.

During the several separations my parents attempted before divorcing, I opted to stay with my father. His reasoning struck me as more logical than Mom's. He certainly knew more of music, sci-fi, and my other preoccupations than she did. I eventually realized in my spiritual evolution that if my father represented knowledge and my mother wisdom, wisdom was the superior of the two. Re-membering the information already stored up in one's soul (Mom's way) trumps the regurgitation of memorized facts (often Dad's approach).

My mother opened Christian World Bookstore in 1982; my first job ever was as a twelve-year-old part-time cashier. She sold bibles, tracts, Christian lit like *The Cross and the Switchblade.* She temporarily taught Sunday school at our church; I fell asleep in her class. Christian World closed in 1984 (the year Dad and I were baptized on Easter Sunday), but we were still connected with the store in the minds of our Trinity Baptist Church congregation. A husband and wife from our church owned the Gun Hill Road bowling alley I rolled strikes at as a shorty, the junior bowling league made up mostly of Sunday school classmates. Pat Robertson's 700 Club mailed us a Christmas card one year, with the Five Percenters I went to school with convincing me that we *were* gods. Taking in the services of several Christian denominational churches after my baptism, I absorbed a great deal alongside my mother in the pews: women flailing around, happy feet dancing, catching the spirit; preachers interpreting messages from women speaking in tongues (the trance-state spiritual language of glossolalia); heard my own mom speak it, in fact; reverends casting out demons.

Before that, though, Mom wrote astrological charts for her friends. (Dad's a Pisces; Mom's an Aquarius. The twentieth century was the Piscean age; the twenty-first is the Aquarian age. This makes me a child of both ages?) She'd read up on faiths outside of the one she'd been born into before deciding Christianity was her choice. So when I began debating her on the downside of organized religion during the late nineties, she already knew the niceties of the argument. Maybe Oprah had something to do with it, but our views on spirituality converged in ways that wouldn't have been possible during the eighties. And without the foundation that those days provided me, overstanding the revelations that have come my way since might have taken longer.

I give thanks to Grandma Benton for my memories of something other than big-city living and rat-race values. I give thanks to Mom for (among so much more) my spiritual foundation. And those records by Labelle, Nina Simone, the Pointer Sisters, Miriam Makeba, Natalie Cole, and Minnie Riperton that she played all the time. The feminine principle rules.

WORLDWIDE UNDERGROUND

S NAPSHOT #1: *Three young black women occupy long stairs leading into the Instituto Internacional en España. One stands, smiling. The other two students sit paging through Madonna's* Sex.

They'd never seen it before, this outrageous limited-edition photo book of Madonna's sex fantasies released just two months ago in the United States. I promised my girlfriend I'd bring my copy (no. 0692054) to Madrid for the amusement of her homegirls. Photographer Steven Meisel's black-and-white shots of Madonna cavorting with Big Daddy Kane and Vanilla Ice say a lot about the spirit of 1992 and induce giggle fits among my present company.

A case study for the perils of being ahead of one's time, the career of Big Daddy Kane took an unpredictable nosedive following the MC's appearance wearing paisley bikini underwear sandwiching Madonna with model Naomi Campbell in *Sex*. Big Daddy Kane rivaled Rakim for emceeing dexterity when "Raw" introduced him in 1988 and his Brooklyn tales of a smooth, suits-and-champagne loverman presaged the narratives of Jay-Z and the Notorious B.I.G. The price of the ticket for going mainstream with his image—posing nude for *Playgirl*, recording music with rhythm-and-blues icons Barry White and Patti Labelle, taking roles in

Hollywood films like *Posse*—cost Big Daddy Kane his core audience. A sacrificial lamb of sorts for hiphop becoming a worldwide youth culture, his story is oddly linked forever in the pages of *Sex* running with a spread directly after his starring Vanilla Ice.

As Spelman study-abroad students snigger at Big Daddy Kane in near embarrassment, the photographs of Vanilla Ice attempting a hiphop James Dean swagger pass nearly unnoticed. Still one of the largest selling rappers of all time, Vanilla Ice, along with MC Hammer, did much for pioneering hiphop's sales dominance during the early 1990s. His rapping was atrocious. Eight million suburban teenagers bought his first album, an audience who couldn't tell the difference, starved for a rapper they resembled with a passable sex-symbol appeal. Interesting, that Madonna's sexual hiphop fantasies should involve an MC slouching towards irrelevance and a rapper who was a punch line to anyone not a gullible, white teenage girl.

SNAPSHOT #2: *Leaning against the arches of the Plaza Mayor, Miles Marshall Lewis wears faded Levi's, black Converse, and a thick flannel shirt with a black wool overcoat.*

I flew to Spain listening to Nirvana, Pearl Jam, and Guns N' Roses; my first tattoo and nose ring both months old. The golden age of hiphop recently ended by 1992 and I took it to heart, exploring the rock music I'd always kept a toehold in anyway. I was still a regional elitist at twenty-one, and popular hiphop from California's Ice Cube and N.W.A held no sway with me. Gangsta rap's misogyny, exaggerated violence, and machismo looked to me like play-acting for the white gaze of hiphop's latest fans. *After years of fad talk, maybe hiphop is finally dying,* I thought. Regretting the slipping quality of the culture's socially conscious music amid the rise of mediocrity (Too Short can't emcee! And is

Arrested Development *really* hiphop?), I decided to sit things out for a spell courtesy of Kurt Cobain and company.

SNAPSHOT #3: *A cobblestone path runs between two treelined blocks that lead to mausoleums and gothic tombstones, some defaced with graf. The most recurring tag is Jim. Some Jims have directional arrows.*

Years passed before I would consider the wrongheadedness of touring a graveyard with a camera in hand. Marcel Proust—*click*. Richard Wright—*click*. Honoré de Balzac—*click*. The Jim tags with their pointers lead visitors of the Père-Lachaise cemetery to the final resting place of the Doors' Jim Morrison. When I get there, freshly strewn flowers lay where Morrison's stolen bust once watched over the area years before. Awake, the graf above his buried body commands.

SNAPSHOT #4: *Standing before a sphinx-like statue with a female head, Miles Marshall Lewis smiles. To his left the wall reads Egyptoman, the letters "ia" cut off by the photo's edge.*

The *Mona Lisa* upstairs doesn't interest me, not with the Louvre featuring African art in their Egyptomania exhibit. A gray cat inspects a dead white chicken, its neck broken, in a Picasso painting; colorful bursts of red and yellow scream out from beneath isolated black capital letters in a larger Miró piece. Entering Egyptomania I tell my friend about a popular hiphop theory on hieroglyphics, that the spirit of the ancient Africans' pictographic script lives on millennia later in the spray-painted tags of graf writers.

"It's not the same," she says.

"Why not? It's both just writing or drawing that's scratched or sprayed on a public surface."

"It's not the same thing."

"But why not?"

She changes the subject.

SNAPSHOT #5: *The Arc de Triomphe shines brilliantly at night-time. The streets of Champs-Élysées glisten slick with rain, streetlamps and car headlights glowing.*

Pariscope says Ravi Coltrane (son of John) plays sax at a club in some arrondissement tonight and that MC Solaar will perform at a club in another venue. With the rain pouring down, my friend and I pass on them both, catching dinner at Foufounes in the Marais quarter instead.

SNAPSHOT #6: *In front of L'as du Fallafel the teenage daughter of the proprietor strikes a pose wearing a jean jacket, sweatpants, and shell-toed Adidas with fat shoelaces.*

The biggest-selling, best-sounding hiphop album around the world in March 1994 belongs to Snoop Dogg—his debut, *Doggystyle*. "Ain't No Fun (If the Homies Can't Have None)" bleats from a portable compact disc player in the small L'as du Fallafel café. The owner prepares an eggplant falafel with hot sauce as my homegirl strikes up conversation with the owner's daughter. Bobbing her head behind the counter, she's clearly responsible for the bistro's hiphop beats.

The daughter knows very little English. Nearly fluent in French, my friend explains to her that in the song's first verse the MC complains of not being able to afford marijuana if he allows himself to care for a woman, also rhyming about passing females along to his friends once he's done having sex with them. The daughter turns to me, disbelieving. Unsure how to communicate the truth of what's just been said, I begin rhyming along with the song, proving that at least I know the lyrics.

I pay for my falafel; we leave. We're halfway down the block before the music shuts off.

I always wondered who silenced Snoop, the girl or her mother.

SNAPSHOT #7: *A burly bouncer planted firmly in front of Subterrania nightclub checks the ID of a young man standing before a long line of multiracial clubheads snaking down the street.*

Reading Terry McMillan novels one after the other, ravenously starved for African-American culture after seven long weeks of living in London, I dog-ear *Disappearing Acts* somewhere in the middle and decide instead on adventure. By one A.M. a black taxicab picks me up at my Belsize Park one-room flat and puts me out in Ladbroke Grove at Subterrania, the de rigueur U.K. hiphop spot circa 1995. A beautiful woman named Timaj dispenses flyers charismatically; the line moves quickly. A flash of my passport and I'm inside, slipping between sweaty Brits jacking bodies to Raekwon's "Criminology." *Much love go to New York City, all my Tommy Hil ice-rocking niggas.* I miss home. Two o'clock, party's over.

SNAPSHOT #8: *D'Angelo tickles the ivories of an organ, supported by three female background singers (Angie Stone in the center). A silhouetted Chaka Khan's voluminous mane is unmistakable in the balcony crowd above.*

The thick cardstock on the table reads RESERVED and we sit anyway, my newfound journalist friend and I, figuring we'll move when absolutely forced to. Soon we are absolutely forced to. Hand-in-hand with Vanessa Paradis, a 'locked Lenny Kravitz sheepishly apologizes ("I didn't want them to put anybody out . . .") as staffers of the Jazz Café scoot us away from their VIP table. "As long as it's you," I manage, downing my third gin and tonic. Standing now, my view is blocked by London native Jazzie B., but thankfully I can peer over the head of his pregnant wife.

Brandishing the confident aura of a cocksure MC,

D'Angelo impresses the audience of his first-ever England appearance with tunes from his debut album, plus cover songs to round out his performance: Al Green's "I'm So Glad You're Mine," Earth, Wind & Fire's "Can't Hide Love," the Ohio Players' "Sweet Sticky Thing." Just last month, August 1995, I missed out on the ticket of the summer—D'Angelo's coming-out party infamous for leaving Prince and T-Boz stranded outside. This night in Camden Town compensates.

SNAPSHOT #9: *Seated behind a bank of keyboards, Miles Marshall Lewis plays chords. A gold record certification plaque for* Kissing to Be Clever *hangs on the wall.*

Kita Craig, the teenage son of Culture Club bassist Michael Craig, rhymes freestyle with me in his friend Giles's forty-eight-track home studio near Hammersmith between passes of a spliff—marijuana mixed with tobacco, British-style. Assembled friends and family in the attic studio pay attention in a drunken, half-past-midnight way until they realize I cannot really rhyme (despite my Bronx lineage).

Giles's girlfriend's schoolmate videotapes an interview with me for a class concerning gangsta rappers and their Mafia obsessions. No ready justifications come to mind. "Rap may get worse before it gets better, and the culture may benefit from being called on its shortcomings by the worldwide hiphop community." Her disappointment at my lack of accountability for my own culture registers, however slightly, in her expression and I feel a bit ashamed.

SNAPSHOT #10: *A blonde museum guide flourishes before tourists in the sculpture garden of Peggy Guggenheim's Palazzo Venier dei Leoni, some taking photographs of the plot where Guggenheim buried her fourteen Shih Tzus.*

The twenty-something museum guide is originally from

New York City. Outside in this garden—formerly a gathering place for the world's artistic elite, Peggy Guggenheim's closest friends and lovers—we strike up a conversation as the crowd dissipates. She takes notice of my headphones.

"Bring any good music with you?"

"Erykah Badu. The new one, *Mama's Gun*."

"Yeah? She's my favorite singer."

SNAPSHOT #11: *A timelessness pervades the moneyed crowd in their forties, fifties, and sixties sitting at tables with snifters and martini glasses, wine and champagne bottles. Some are noticeably drunk.*

During the mid-twentieth century Harry's Bar, in the San Marco section of Venice, for years served Ernest Hemingway his favorite drink of nine parts gin, one part martini. I sit at a table with an ex-girlfriend from Paris, downing a shot of Hemingway's poison.

"I feel like I'm a little late to the party," I say.

"Late?" says my English-challenged ex, Christine.

"I feel like Hemingway and I would've had this drink here together fifty years ago. I feel like I would've had conversations with Peggy Guggenheim yesterday in her garden at the museum with Picasso, Jackson Pollock. Maybe I'd smoke a joint with her daughter Pegeen. I'm a little late to the party, through no fault of my own. Artists travel far and wide leaving our marks behind. I feel like I'm planting a flag for hiphop right now, up in Hemingway's hangout with all these old heads."

"Ha! Hiphop is in the record store down the street. It's here already."

"You don't even get what I'm saying, Frenchie. How 'bout another round?"

"You *'ricain—tu m'énerves!*"

SNAPSHOT #12: *Dozens of pigeons flock around Christine Herelle, lining her arm to eat seeds from her hand in the Piazza San Marco.*

Pigeons fed, we troop forward to the Basilica di San Marco and I point upward.

"Funny how everything in that place was plundered by the Moors in Africa," I say. "In a thousand years hiphop could be jacked just like this, with some other culture claiming our shit revisionist-style. Just watch."

"But I like Eminem," she says, reviving an inside joke.

We both laugh.

II. THE DEF OF HIPHOP

PEACE, UNITY, LOVE, HAVING FUN

KOOL HERC WEPT.
Presented by the Universal Zulu Nation with a plaque for his pioneering achievements as the father of hiphop, Clive Campbell a/k/a Kool DJ Herc—tears streaming from his eyes—shocks those assembled in the South Bronx at the Skate Key. Nearly six-and-a-half feet (the sobriquet "Herc" is short for the towering Greek god Hercules), Kool Herc loses his footing in grief, toppling backward into the waiting arms of a Zulu King. The ceremony thereby cut short, a phalanx of well-wishers begin to follow Kool Herc—composing himself—offstage. The beats from DJ Kayslay resuming his expert turntablism soon reverberate throughout the hall.

THERE CAN BE NO MORE authentic a hiphop fête in procession anywhere on earth this Saturday night than the Ultimate Throwback Jerzee Party. The Skate Key is separated into two huge skating rinks constituting two wholly separate areas. Teenagers too young for true nightclubs inundate one area dancing to fleeting popular songs of the moment: "Hot in Herre," "Jenny From the Block," "Bonnie & Clyde '02." No one, apparently, can name the DJ. Celebration for the twenty-eighth anniversary of hiphop culture and the twenty-ninth anniversary of the Universal Zulu Nation takes place in the other area, past the ID checkpoint. For adults only, vendors sell Zulu Nation T-shirts; legendary (circa 1977) Bronx-park DJ sets by the L Brothers and GrandWizzard Theodore transferred from dusty cassettes to compact discs; tomes like *Yes Yes Y'all* by Jim Fricke and Charlie Ahearn and *Back in the Days* by Jamel Shabazz; oral histories and pictorials documenting the most embryonic period of what was briefly coined B-beat music—what would eventually become known as hiphop culture. Mixing records behind two turntables to the far right of the stage, about one hundred feet away from those hawking his park jams from twenty-five years ago, stands Theodore Livingston a/k/a GrandWizzard Theodore.

Crowding an area meant for roller skaters are dozens of B-boys and B-girls of various nationalities and ages dressed in T-shirts, sneakers, jeans, and vinyl sweatpants; some tweeners, some forty-somethings, some African American, some Caribbean, some Latino, all reacting to the records selected by the DJ. Legendary B-boys like Pee Wee Dance and Frosty Freeze execute headspins, backspins, and other dance moves within a circle of onlookers to the sonic backdrop of "Bongo Rock," "Give It Up or Turnit a Loose," and more. Relieving GrandWizzard Theodore, famed Kool DJ Red Alert keeps up the flow of breakbeat tunes. A Japanese B-girl uprocks then windmills to "It's Just Begun." The turntable needle skips occasionally, to the dancers' collective consternation. No one attending the Ultimate Throwback Jerzee Party in this section of the Skate Key is doing, say, the Harlem shake or any other modern, trendy dance of the day. On this dance floor, there are spectators and B-boys, only.

The strictest adherents of the culture have celebrated November as Hiphop History Month since 1974. The world's oldest, largest, and most respected hiphop organization—the

Universal Zulu Nation—cites its own birthday as November 12, 1973, and the birthday of hiphop itself as November 12, 1974. "That's when we officially started using the termnology 'hiphop' on a mass level," says Zulu Nation founder Afrika Bambaataa. "Before '73 there was no name for this. Some people just [called it] 'boing-oing-oing,' some 'bebop'— taken from the forties jazz-type thing, 'bebop swing' and all that. The Zulu Nation got its foundation in '73 and then we decided in '74, on that same date, we gonna start pushing hiphop. I took the [term 'hiphop'] from a brother named Lovebug Starski. We basically was planning to organize it. DJs that came after Herc, myself, and [Grandmaster] Flash, they wasn't thinking about no culture. They wasn't thinking about organizing."

As of December 12, 2002, the New York State Senate also recognizes November as Hiphop History Month. The official proclamation reads:

> Whereas, it is the sense of this legislative body that those who enhance the well-being and vitality of their community and have shown a long and sustained commitment to excellence certainly have earned our recognition and applause; now, therefore, be it resolved that this legislative body pause in its deliberations to honor the rich traditions of hiphop culture. The month of November is now recognized by the State of New York as Hiphop Culture History Month.

On the night of November 9, a month prior to the New York Senate's recognition, a couple hundred celebrants honor hiphop at the Skate Key. Middle-aged black women pass out paper plates of soul food near the vendor tables in the back. Nowhere near the amount of revelers are assembled for this celebration as might have attended the opening of Sean Combs's restaurant Justin's or Jay-Z's 40/40 Club. Rap music as promoted on MTV and the hiphop culture which birthed the music genre are not synonymous. Teenagers screaming for celebrity rappers like Fabolous on *Total Request Live* (MTV's popular twenty-first-century version of *American Bandstand*) would be unmoved by hiphop legends like the Almighty KayGee walking among them in the flesh at the Skate Key. A large angel food cake is cut; more paper plates are passed with plastic flatware. Flanked by a few Amazulus (members of the Zulu Nation), Afrika Bambaataa moves slowly, making his way past the food and vendors, past the rink riddled with popping, locking B-boys, past DJ Kayslay spinning "Dance to the Drummer's Beat," and onto the stage. The music stops.

Afrika Bambaataa is introduced. Dressed in African regalia, holding a plaque in his arms, he resembles Moses on the mount missing a tablet. At the microphone stand Afrika Bambaataa speaks of his respect and love for Kool DJ Herc, and the debt owed by the Universal Zulu Nation and hiphop worldwide to the man who set the style of hiphop in the early 1970s: introducing breakbeats on his Herculord sound system with huge speakers in Bronx community centers; featuring early MCs like Coke La Rock of the Herculoids rapping rhymes atop Herc's deejayed rhythms; coining the term "B-boy," meaning "Bronx boy" or "break boy" for those who dance to breakbeats. Afrika Bambaataa delivers a brief, rehearsed history of hiphop culture—tracing it back to African-American antecedents like Moms Mabley, Cab Calloway, Ella Fitzgerald, Pigmeat Markham, Malcolm X, and the Last Poets—then presents his award to Kool DJ Herc.

The father of hiphop hugs the godfather of hiphop and accepts his plaque. Applause rises and falls. Kool Herc says he is often asked his opinion on the state of hiphop and responds, "Hiphop is beautiful!" He says that pundits outside of the culture who have no abiding interest in hiphop or the inner city that invented it expect him to denounce its ills or air its dirty laundry. Kool Herc advises hiphop's founding figures assembled scattershot in the audience to hang on to their photographs and party flyers from the early 1970s, warning them against commercial exploitation. He condemns the books being sold in the back of the venue commemorating hiphop's earliest days, complaining that he receives no profits from these products bearing his likeness and capitalizing on his contributions, specifically indicting author and filmmaker Charlie Ahearn. (*Yes Yes Y'all*, coauthored by Ahearn and Jim Fricke, features Herc dressed in a sheepskin coat on the back cover of its dust jacket and quotes him inside.) Wending back to the subject of the state of hiphop culture, Kool Herc mentions the late Jason Mizell a/k/a DJ Jam Master Jay of Run-D.M.C., how he wishes his brother were still alive. Ten days ago an unknown assailant in Queens, New York, shot Jam Master Jay at point-blank range.

Kool Herc pauses. He raises his hand to eyes welled with tears and begins to ball. He spits out a few more words on the murder of Jam Master Jay, then his emotions overtake him completely and he nearly collapses. Amazulus lead him off the stage. And the DJ plays on.

OVER THREE DECADES AGO, a Blimpie stood on the corner of Bruckner Boulevard and Feteley Street in the South Bronx. Written with a fat marker on the yellow wall in late-sixties-style crude graffiti were the names of the eleven founding members of the Black Spades. A Bronx street gang initially founded in 1968 as the Savage Seven, the Black Spades would mushroom from eleven core members to several hundred, encompassing forty-eight divisions citywide. The origins of cliques (an identifying term much preferred by all Bronx gangs of the era) like the Black Spades have largely been lost to time. Those who tell don't know, those who know don't tell, and the rest are either dead, jailed, or have been promising autobiographies for umpteen years now. The historical thread of the Bronx cliques' murky past is something of a two-headed hydra. By one account cliques formed in reaction to a proliferation of drug pushers and addicts in ghetto neighborhoods circa 1967–1970, street vigilantes policing against the widespread presence of heroin. Another account posits the cliques as preying on their own neighbors, dangerously armed and warring with rival cliques in an urbanized Wild West scenario. Reconciling the two divergent histories may be impossible.

Trace the legacy of the Universal Zulu Nation backwards in time—through incarnations like the Mighty Zulu Nation, the Zulu Nation, the Organization, and the Bronx River Organization—and you will eventually reach the Black Spades and its one-time warlord Afrika Bambaataa. "I usually don't speak on Black Spades history until I'm ready to do my whole book on that," Afrika Bambaataa says diplomatically, seated in an office at the National Black Theatre in Harlem—the current headquarters of the Universal Zulu Nation at One Hundred Twenty-fifth Street and Fifth Avenue. "Black Spades' motto was to basically kick ass," he laughs, "cause destruction and kick ass. We used to bust the drug dealers on they asses. 'Get the hell out of our communities!' You had crazy serious drug wars with the drug dealers at the time."

Cliques ousting heroin dealers is a matter of public record. The *New York Post*—in a six-part series on New York City street gangs—reported on June 26, 1972:

After addicts robbed and stabbed an eighty-three-year-old resident of Minford Place two years ago . . . the Turbans spread the word that addicts were no longer welcome on Minford, beat up a few to stress their seriousness, posted "Junkies Keep Out" signs decorated with the skull-and-crossbones, and started patrolling the block.

Half a year later, January 16, 1973, the *New York Times* relayed:

Members of a clique called the Secret Bachelors have been arrested in the murder of a thirty-seven-year-old drug pusher whose body was found on Prospect Avenue riddled with six bullet holes in the shape of a cross.

New York Times reporter Gary Hoenig published *Reaper* in the mid-1970s, a memoir of a former president of the fourth division Reapers. Hoenig wrote:

At first the gangs directed their attention to drug traffic, waging a private war on pushers big and small, enacting and sometimes enforcing, with a vengeance, strict hard-drug taboos on their memberships. A few junkies would be tossed off rooftops or down elevator shafts, or shot in the face, or stabbed in the groin. By early 1970, the gangs had partially succeeded in pushing drug traffic west across Third Avenue.

Research pop culture for an analogous formulation and its best to skip over the Fonz and *West Side Story* and head straight to the Korova Milkbar crew of *A Clockwork Orange* or the Five Corners mobs of Martin Scorsese's *Gangs of New York*. New York City gangs like the Fordham Baldies and Egyptian Kings of the 1950s—with their rumbles, leather jackets, and zip guns made from metal tubes and wooden sticks—died out largely due to the heroin addiction of their members. The Bronx began to breed a new strain of street gang as teenage Vietnam War veterans returned to the inner city with uniquely military kill-or-be-killed skills, coming home to neighborhoods decimated by Parks Commissioner Robert Moses's construction of the Cross Bronx Expressway and the white flight that ensued, slumlords' absentee regulation of tenement buildings with faulty heat, gas, and electricity abounding. Dog packs roamed the desolate streets during the nighttime hours. Returning from class to 1595 East One Hundred Seventy-fourth Street and Stratton Avenue, building eight in the Bronx River Houses project, a teenage student began tagging Bambaataa 117 on brick walls in the late 1960s, noticing the reality of his surroundings changing daily.

Sampling the sartorial style of motorcycle gangs like the Hell's Angels, cliques in the Bronx began sporting denim jackets (called "colors") with the sleeves torn away, ornate lettering and designs emblazoned across the back. Seven Immortals jackets featured a left hand tightly grasping a lightning bolt embossed over the number seven; Cypress Bachelors wore the likeness of a top hat and cane stitched to their jackets; the Black Spades' simple logo was the black spade of a playing card with a skull in the center, staring. A triumvirate assumed leadership of the cliques: a president, a vice president, and a warlord in charge of disputes with other cliques. Many remixes of hiphop history attribute Afrika Bambaataa as "leader" of the Black Spades, and by this term the uninformed authors seem to mean president. But the man himself says he was a warlord, one of the possible misconceptions he refuses to clarify. "When I'm ready to write my book, then you'll get to the factology of the thing," Afrika Bambaataa says, laughing.

The Black Spades' turf spread from the Bronx River Parkway on the west to the beginning of Throgs Neck on the east. The clique convened weekly meetings at the Soundview project's community center. Many Bronx gangs elected against a headquarters, deciding it best not to congregate in one known area lest the police come calling. Others disagreed— the Savage Skulls could be found in a clubhouse at 1038 Tiffany Street; the Royal Javelins in a basement room at 1438 Vyse Avenue; and the Ghetto Brothers in a storefront at 880 East One Hundred Sixty-second Street.

Bronx gang lore boasts a few must-mentions. One concerns the Family Peace Treaty of 1971. In August 1970 Ted Gross was appointed the deputy commissioner of the Youth Services Agency, a division of the Human Resources Administration of New York City. Sometime during 1971 Eduardo Vincenti—a worker for the Bronx crisis squad of the Youth Services Agency—hatched the idea of coalescing the city's disparate cliques into a single gang, subject to an intergang nonviolence treaty. While drafting the treaty, Gross inexplicably transferred Vincenti from the Bronx to Brooklyn, where he was shot in the face attempting to prevent a gun battle in the West Farms area. (Vincenti survived; Bronx crisis squad employees suspected Gross's involvement.) Nevertheless, on December 8, 1971, six days following the murder of Ghetto Brothers ambassador Cornell "Black Benjie" Benjamin—clubbed to death while interceding in a gang battle—Eduardo Vincenti was able to convene twenty-six cliques at the Bronx Boys Club on Hoe Avenue to sign the Family Peace Treaty. Within months, sixty-eight gang presidents became signatories.

By summertime the Treaty had fallen apart. Still, intergang alliances already existed without the prodding of the Human Resources Administration. The Javelins, the Reapers, the Young Sinners, and the Peacemakers had already formed a coalition called the Brotherhood; likewise, the Black Spades forged an unofficial alliance with the Savage Nomads, the Seven Immortals, and the Savage Skulls.

"We meet in the streets with our brothers all the time," new Ghetto Brothers president Benjie Melendez told the *New York Post*. "We don't have to go to places that are controlled by other people." Come February 1973, Ted Gross had been sentenced to three years in jail, found guilty on two counts of accepting kickbacks.

Another mentionable concerns war between the Black Spades and the Secret and Imperial Bachelors. According to an article in the June 17, 1973 *New York Times,* four gang members forced three of their rivals to line up against a four-story building at 329 East One Hundred Forty-fifth Street. The four, armed with pistols and a rifle, opened fire on the defenseless three. The following day a hail of gunfire rained down on three teens reportedly returning home from their jobs; two gun-wielding gang members were held responsible. "The toll was one dead, three wounded," said the *New York Times*. "[T]he street version is that the shootings were part of a war between two of the largest gangs, the Bachelors and the Black Spades, stemming from a Bachelor hold-up of a Spade-protected drug pusher." A Spade-protected drug pusher? History has it that the gangs hated heroin but were softer on marijuana. Yet this doesn't sound quite right. Author Gary Hoenig corroborates in *Reaper*:

> [T]wo Bronx mobsters were on the verge of warring with each other over drug territory in the southeast Bronx. Both recognized the costs involved in such a war . . . So they simply subcontracted the entire war. One mob hired the Black Spades; the other hired the Secret and Imperial Bachelors. The shooting reached the point where seven kids were gunned down within thirty-six hours, though only one died. All were lined up execution style against building walls and shot with high-caliber rifles.

Not all gangland stories fit snugly into hiphop history. What is worse, writes Gary Hoenig, "Within a few months, Bachelor and Spade divisions all over the Bronx were at war with one another. That war brought . . . deaths due to street-gang activity to the highest level yet recorded." (*Reaper* was published in 1975.)

On the subject of hiphop revisionist history, a story Afrika Bambaataa agrees to discuss involves Soulski. False legend credits the murder of a friend named Soulski as the cause of Afrika Bambaataa transitioning the Black Spades into the Zulu Nation. The story he shares is more compli-cated. "Yeah, well, a brother who got killed by the police officers of Pelham Bay by the name of Soulski, he was one of the leaders of the tenth division Black Spades," Afrika Bambaataa begins. "They did him in and a couple of other Spades, and almost caused a lot of friction between the Spades and the government officials—like firemen, police officers, and all that. He was uniting gangs to go against them. It was certain people from the *Amsterdam News* who came and tried to talk the brothers down from making a mistake, thinking they could take on the police. And then the Nation of Islam became involved. When he got killed I think it was '75."

Another misconception to creep into hiphop history holds that Afrika Bambaataa disbanded the Black Spades as he established the more community-minded Bronx River Organization in 1972. "The Bronx River Organization was first started to get Bronx River [Houses] more organized for any frictions," he says. "You know, a lot of our projects had frictions in-between a building and a building or this project don't like that project. So when I started the Bronx River Organization, that's when the gangs were starting to slack down and I needed something to keep going. It was really [made up of] the Black Spades, the Savage Skulls, the Savage

Nomads. And that's the basis that made up the Zulu Nation." Though gang activity diminished toward the mid-1970s, it did not completely disappear. A January 12, 1974 *New York Times* article reported:

[M]embers of the Black Spades were taken without incident after police officers burst into the sparsely furnished fourth-floor apartment where they stayed. A sawed-off twelve-gauge shotgun, a .30-caliber rifle, several rounds of ammunition, and some machetes and baseball bats were among the weapons recovered, the police said.

Two months later—March 21—the *New York Times* informed:

[T]hirteen alleged members of the Black Spades and one member of the Peacemakers were arrested after the police saw them apparently on their way to fight.

And even a full year afterwards—January 7, 1975—the *New York Times* wrote:

Two young armed men were killed and a shotgun-carrying member of a Bronx youth gang was seriously wounded last night by police gunfire touched off when the victims attempted to flee during a routine traffic check near the Bronx Zoo. Before the three men were shot, they had pointed loaded weapons at the officers, police said . . . The other man was identified as twenty-year-old James Wilder, a member of the Black Spades youth gang.

In less than a year, gripes among members prompted Afrika Bambaataa to drop the "Bronx River" prefix from the Organization. "I started uniting all the projects in the southeast Bronx under the banner 'the Bronx River Organization': Monroe Houses, Soundview, Castle Hill, Patterson projects, and a lot of other areas. We had a big meeting in our old center and a lot of people was complaining. 'Why we using the name Bronx River? Everybody ain't from Bronx River.' No problem. We started changing it to 'the Organization,' and everybody agreed on that. They went a span for two-and-a-half years. And at this same time, we also started the Zulu Nation, which was starting in Adlai E. Stevenson High School and Bronx River Houses at the same time."

Thus, under the direct inspiration of Shaka—one of the greatest leaders of recorded African history—and his 1817 creation of the Zulu nation in southeast Africa, Afrika Bambaataa birthed the South Bronx's own Zulu Nation in 1973.

DYNAMITE J'S BREAKDOWN of the term "hiphop" from Zulunation.com is the officially sanctioned explanation:

> Where did the name "hiphop" come from, and who is responsible for saying the name "hiphop" came from Afrika Bambaataa? When Bam throws a party, he feels like a theme name for his party would be better and more exciting . . . One of the names for his early parties was The Hiphop Beeny Bop. Some could equate this as a teen jam because of the phrase "beeny bop." Bop is also short for boppers.
>
> So when Bambaataa had his parties, and [Lovebug] Starski would emcee the jam, he would say things like, "Welcome to the Hiphop Beeny Bop! That's right y'all, hiphop till you don't stop!" So true respect is given to MC Starski with being credited for popularizing the phrase "hiphop," but it's also respect and credit due to Afrika Bambaataa for starting the word "hiphop."

According to Bambaataa, the Zulu Nation began "saying 'elements' in hiphop, started pooling the culture together: the B-boys, the MCs, the graffiti artists, [the DJs], and gave you your fifth element, the knowledge. We used it in 1974 when we started really pushing it strongly as 'hiphop,' as a culture. So we coined this word and I took it, decided to name it for the culture, started using it a lot in the Zulu Nation."

This is a literary needle drop. Some DJs possess the ability to drop the turntable's stylus onto a record with blasé panache, landing the needle directly into the grooves of a song's breakbeat beginning; the technique was yet another innovation of GrandWizzard Theodore. I am likewise lifting my micro Faber-Castell from Afrika Bambaataa's 1974 Hiphop Beeny Bop and dropping its rolling uni-ball back down in 1982 at downtown Manhattan's trendy Mudd Club. This is no history of hiphop. Other volumes have been there and done that effectively with a variety of styles: *Hip Hop America* by Nelson George; *Black Noise* by Tricia Rose. This essay deals with the origin and legacy of the Zulu Nation and its founder, which by definition details the historical essence of hiphop culture. But this composition does not claim responsibility for describing the minutiae of hiphop's illustrious thirty-year history to date. We'll be here all day.

So. In addition to grouping the distinct cultural elements of breaking emceeing aerosol art and deejaying under the newly named rubric of hiphop Afrika Bambaataa also instituted a motto for the Zulu Nation and by extension hiphop—"peace unity love and having fun"—as the style of deejaying trailblazed by Kool Herc Afrika Bambaataa and Grandmaster Flash started to seep from the Bronx into nightclubs in the upper Manhattan neighborhoods of Harlem and Washington Heights where the Harlem World-performing Lovebug Starkski attracted the attention of former rhythm-and-blues singer Sylvia Robinson (of "Pillow Talk" fame) who decided to put together a trio of rappers from New Jersey name them the Sugarhill Gang record them rapping over the instrumental to Chic's current hit "Good Times" (with rhymes actually "borrowed" from the Cold Crush Brothers' Grandmaster Caz p/k/a Casanova Fly without attribution or financial retribution) and name it "Rapper's Delight" in July 1979 to the chagrin of Bronx MCs which nonetheless commercialized hiphop and sparked a chain of events resulting in Afrika Bambaataa recording the seminal "Planet Rock" three years later with the Soulsonic Force of MCs comprised of Zulu Nation members Pow Wow Mr. Biggs and G.L.O.B.E.

(Here comes the needle drop.)

Fab 5 Freddy told me everybody's fly
DJ spinning, I said "my-my"
Flash is fast, Flash is cool
François c'est pas Flashé non due
And you don't stop, sure shot
—Debbie Harry, "Rapture"

ELEMENTS OF HIPHOP, particularly emceeing, swiftly became commodities following the culture's introduction to the white populace of American society during the early 1980s. "Rapper's Delight" across radio airwaves was the watershed event; seen as faddish novelties, in 1979 and 1980 Kurtis Blow's singles "Christmas Rappin'" and "The Breaks" soon appeared, as well as 1979's "Superappin'" by Grandmaster Flash and the Furious Five, and several other rap singles. The burgeoning music scene of downtown Manhattan (e.g., CBGB featuring punk and new wave bands like Television and the Talking Heads) was just hip enough to appreciate hiphop. A fixture in that germinating world, Debbie Harry of Blondie acknowledged both Grandmaster Flash and graf artist Fred "Fab 5 Freddy" Brathwaite in a credible rhyme smack-dab in the middle of Blondie's 1980 "Rapture." (Fresh from tagging Samo© on subway trains, painter Jean-Michel Basquiat famously appears in the promotional video for the song. The artist would later be credited with producing "Beat Bop" for graf writer Rammelzee and Bronx MC K-Rob in 1983, friends immortalized in his *Hollywood Africans* painting of the same year.) The Mudd Club at 77 White Street, just south of the Canal Street thoroughfare, served as the cool-dive anti–Studio 54 hangout for those downtown hipsters. The four-story loft space hosted Afrika Bambaataa in 1982, the first time the DJ spun for a predominately white crowd.

"The punk rock whites was the first to accept hiphop," Afrika Bambaataa recalls. "They was the most boldest whites that wasn't scared to come to party with blacks and Latinos up in the Bronx. The Asians had started coming in the eighties. Everybody started coming more in the eighties when it was okay and cool to do so. In the seventies they ain't really, 'cause it woulda caused problems then. They still had their racist mentality thinking." The Mudd Club appearance of Afrika Bambaataa was among many downtown hiphop cultural exchanges. "Wheels of Steel Night started at Negril," remembers Richie Colón a/k/a Crazy Legs, President of the Rock Steady Crew breaking outfit. "It started at Negril then it went to Danceteria. That led to the Roxy. Mudd Club was just a different party."

First downtown New York City, then Europe. Hiphop stormed the international stage in November 1982 courtesy of promoter Kool Lady Blue and cosponsors Europe 1 and Fnac department stores; the New York City Rap Tour hit Paris, London, Lyon, Metz, Belfort, Strasbourg, and

Milhouse, with Zulu Nation members Fab 5 Freddy, Grandmixer D.XT, Phase 2, Mr. Freeze, Dondi White, Crazy Legs, and Futura 2000 all in tow. Deejaying for French teenagers in Le Bataclan concert hall and Le Palace carried an immense significance when measured against the community center parties of the Bronx River Houses a decade earlier.

Drumming his brain for memories of Europeans' first reactions to hiphop, Crazy Legs says, "The thing that stands out most—besides our wild antics in the hotel and all that shit—was, we were in Paris and we were performing. The [World Champion Fantastic Four] Double Dutch girls were on the stage at the time, and this one person threw a bottle at one of the girls. Then D.XT came out wildin off the stage. We all just grabbed our belts with the nameplate buckle and wrapped 'em around our hands. D.XT and I forget who else ran into the audience and beat the shit out of the dude. Yeah. And after they got back onstage the audience started clapping."

(Another needle drop . . .)

Me sweat another?
I do my own thing
Strictly hardcore tracks
Not a new jack swing
—Phife, "Jazz (We've Got)"

FROM ITS ORIGINS IN THE BLACK SPADES warring against rival gangs, the Universal Zulu Nation would establish a reputation as a peacekeeping force in hiphop during the 1990s—no surprise given the culture's position as a constant hotbed of irony and contradiction. The Zulu Nation's first such intervention stemmed from the above cited lines of Phife, partner to Q-Tip of A Tribe Called Quest. A member of rap group Wreckx-N-Effect assaulted Q-Tip in 1993 as the result of a perceived slight inferred from Phife's rhyme. A musical style innovated by record producer (and Wreckx-N-Effect svengali) Teddy Riley, "new jack swing" melded hiphop to rhythm and blues in a fashion Phife sought to distance A Tribe Called Quest from in his characteristically dismissive rap style. Zulu Nation member Q-Tip involved Afrika Bambaataa and the Nation of Islam in mediating their dispute before things could escalate beyond his blackened eye.

By 1995 the Universal Zulu Nation had established chapters worldwide in Japan, Germany, and the same South Africa where its namesake was founded in the early nineteenth century. Yet, unimpressed by these credentials, the New York City Housing Authority brought about bureaucratic changes that year which led to the ousting of the Zulu Nation from their Bronx River Houses headquarters of over two decades. Operation of the housing project was transferred from the New York City Housing Authority to the newly formed Bronx River Community Center Inc., half of whose membership resided in the nine-building complex. In a change of policy, the Zulu Nation was banned from convening meetings at the Bronx River Houses center where Afrika Bambaataa had united the community at parties in the early 1970s, due to a lack of resident status. Longstanding graf was soon washed from the walls. Further, changes in federal law now classified the Universal Zulu Nation as a gang (!), allowing the New York City Housing Authority to prohibit them from using the facility.

"[Mayor Rudy Guiliani] sent his patrolmens to try to get us outta there," Afrika Bambaataa says. "Everybody think they chased us outta there. We just stepped out of it, Bronx River Houses. We told the area, 'If you not gonna fight for what's yours, then we gon' move on.' I had everybody meet downtown where we marched on City Hall. And they got nervous 'cause I told them we was coming with three states full of people, but I hit them in their pocket 'cause I really came with about five hundred. But they had sharpshooters, they had S.W.A.T. teams, the train conductors was police agents. They had the people on horseback and the scooters, they was crazy. I hit them to make them spend money." That May 1995 march on City Hall—attended by the Reverends Al Sharpton and Calvin Butts as well as a sizable segment of the Nation of Islam—still ended in the Zulu Nation relinquishing their Bronx home base, reestablishing themselves at Harlem's National Black Theatre.

ONE TENDS TO SEE THE SAME FACES at celebrations for hiphop's foundation. Onstage at the Manhattan Center standing atop a graf-adorned 6 train behind two turntables and a microphone is Kool DJ Red Alert. (The 6 train is actually a cardboard façade.) Stepping out onto the linoleum center floor, breaking to Main Source and EPMD records in direct view of surrounding B-boy crews, is Frosty Freeze. Underneath a banner proclaiming the twenty-seventh anniversary of the Rock Steady Crew stands Afrika Bambaataa, speaking jovially with Rock Steady Crew President Crazy Legs.

Sweltering summertime heat dominates the New York City streets this July afternoon, but inside the Manhattan Center the air-conditioning slowly subjects revelers to a Freon-powered variant of water torture. The evening won't be old before DJs compete in a world supremacy championship, breaking crews battle for a coveted title, and MC Keith Murray stagedives into a crowd holding him aloft with the sampled beat of George McCrae's "I Get Lifted" blaring. At the time of the Zulu Nation's 1973 inception, five B-boys known as the Shaka Zulu Kings manifested the organization's breaking arm along with the Shaka Zulu Queens; in 1982 the Rock Steady Crew joined the Zulu Nation as an affiliate group and tonight marks the final day of their weekend anniversary festivities.

Resting alongside vendor tables selling T-shirts ("F*ck you, I rhyme better," they proclaim) and sipping a Lipton iced tea (a cosponsor of the Rock Steady Crew anniversary) Kool DJ Red Alert—longstanding Zulu Nation member, one-time DJ in Afrika Bambaataa's Soulsonic Force, and twenty-year veteran DJ on the New York City radio circuit—speaks of whom many have nicknamed the Master of Records. "I got down with the Zulu Nation in the year of '79," Red Alert says. "My cousin [DJ] Jazzy Jay, he got down with the Zulu Nation before me 'cause he moved from Manhattan up in the Bronx, the Bronx River projects. He bought his own set of turntables, started getting his own set of records, cutting up and doing things in the house. The person who really acknowledged him first before Bam was—may he rest in peace—Disco King Mario. Then Bam said, 'Well, where he from?' 'Yo, Bam, he from here.' 'What is he doin over *there*? He supposed to be with us!' But at the same time, Bam had two other DJs named Zombu and Sinbad. One of them had pulled out and then Jazzy came in. Afterwards, Jazzy used to speak so much to Bam about me that Bam took interest and put me in."

Inspired by the Bronx jams of Kool DJ D, DJ Tex, and particularly Kool DJ Herc (they shared many of the same records in common), Afrika Bambaataa inaugurated his own deejaying style in the early 1970s by reaching for the truly obscure and diverse. Speeches from Malcolm X and Martin Luther King Jr. were draped over Soweto drums, sharing earspace with the television themes to *The Andy Griffith Show*, *Batman*, and *The Pink Panther*, playing in a set list including the eclectic likes of Kraftwerk's "Trans-Europe Express," Fela

Anikulapo-Kuti's "Shakara," and various Bugs Bunny cartoons.

"His legacy is showing the diversity of music," agrees Red Alert. "He went after different scriptures of sound, different from everybody else. Bam went after sounds that people would never even think of, but he had some type of way of grabbing the certain sound that had an Afrocentric feeling to it—from the congos, drums, or anything in that sense that relates to within Africa."

Afrika Bambaataa admits, "I just was crazy as a music lover. I would even play records that might be thirty-three [revolutions per minute] and speed it up to forty-five, or a record that might be a forty-five and slow it down to a thirty-three. I took commercials off of TV and added breakbeats to it and played it at the party with astral tapes. My audience was already progressive-minded, they just was with me whatever I was gonna do. We started [playing] a lot of rock, added a lot of salsa records, African records, calypso records and stuff. Wherever I could get beats and funky grooves from."

My uncle Craig—who attended classes at Edmund Rice High School with Run-D.M.C.'s Darryl "D.M.C." McDaniels—often returned from school in the late seventies with three-to-ten-dollar cassette tapes of Afrika Bambaataa parties and DJ battles; these tapes circulated widely among cab drivers, students, and party people. Most famous of Afrika Bambaataa's sound system opponents included the late Disco King Mario, Grandmaster Caz, Grandmaster Flash, and Kool DJ Herc. A Zulu Nation jam recorded live at James Monroe High School in the Bronx during 1980 sold three years later as Paul Winley Records' *Death Mix Live!!*, a poorly recorded, nearly twenty-minute mix by Afrika Bambaataa and DJ Jazzy Jay. (The same year, Paul Winley Records also recorded "Zulu Nation Throwdown," credited to Afrika Bambaataa Zulu Nation Cosmic Force.)

After attending an Afrika Bambaataa party, Tom Silverman—of *Dance Music Report* magazine, later the founder of Tommy Boy Records—struck up a friendship with the DJ that flowered into a business relationship in 1981. "We did 'Let's Vote' with Cotton Candy," Afrika Bambaataa says, "and then after that came the 'Jazzy Sensation,'" credited to Afrika Bambaataa & the Jazzy 5, of which DJ Jazzy Jay and Kool DJ Red Alert were members. Then came the seminal "Planet Rock."

"Afrika Bambaataa, Arthur Baker, and John Robie had all grind up together to make this, as Bam had in his mind the idea to create this record," Red Alert remembers. "Like I always said, Bam is ahead of everybody. And when that record he made came out, it was different from everywhere else. And that was the start of electro-funk. Right after that record, how many other dance and rap records sound similar to it? 'Jam on It' [by Newcleus], it's a host of them. It's that electro-funk stage, that sound. It went on down further south and went out west. In the South they loved it but they sped it up and added more bottom to it. It became bass records, you know? That was a record that helped really create a lot of things in the music industry. Not just for in rap, but I'm talking about the whole industry in general."

Afrika Bambaataa explains, "The reason why I made electro-funk hiphop is because I looked around [and] there was no group nowhere whatsoever that was doing strictly electronic music like Kraftwerk, Electric Music Orchestra with Gary Neuman. And I said, 'Well, we gonna be the first with this.' So I took the idea of what they had with the techno-pop, what Electric Music Orchestra was calling it, what they was doing, and adding that funk to it, the basis of James Brown, Sly, and P-Funk. Put it to our stuff and took the style of dressing from Sly and P-Funk to build up the electro-funk and hiphop."

The 1982 release of "Planet Rock" solidified Afrika Bambaataa's standing in the music industry—from Black Spades warlord to Zulu Nation founder to the emissary of a worldwide cultural revolution and owner of a gold record, within a decade's time. "Looking for the Perfect Beat" followed shortly on Tommy Boy Records in 1983. Former Sex Pistols singer John Lydon recorded with Afrika Bambaataa and Time Zone (a group Bambaataa helped develop on the Celluloid Records label) on "World Destruction" in 1984, a collaboration of hiphop and rock predating "Walk This Way" with Run-D.M.C. and Aerosmith by two years.

That same 1984, which found the Rock Steady Crew performing at an inauguration for the late President Ronald Reagan, the godfather of hiphop met the godfather of soul: "Unity, Part 1" featured James Brown and Afrika Bambaataa exhorting in unison, "Peace, unity, love, and having fun," the fundamental creed of the Universal Zulu Nation. "Funk You!" by Afrika Bambaataa & Family came in 1985, leading to an invitation to appear on "Sun City," an anti-apartheid charity single including luminaries like Miles Davis, Bruce Springsteen, Pete Townshend, and Bono.

In the nineties Afrika Bambaataa revisited the marriage of music and activism as a hiphop veteran, co-organizing a concert for the African National Congress at London's Wembley Stadium with John Baker and Greenstreet Records in honor of Nelson Mandela's release from prison. The benefit single "Ndodemnyama (Free South Africa)" helped raise thirty thousand dollars for the African National Congress.

"Africa was no joke," relates Afrika Bambaataa. "A lot of people, I be telling: 'You need to get back to Africa. Do shows.' I been there a couple of times. They say that everybody talk Africa but don't come to do shows or nothing in Africa. That's why my goal was to go all over the world and rake this music into many countries. People think hiphop just sprang and everybody started loving it. It was a lot of work going from country to country, many times. It took me a lot of work to go to each country, city, playing cafés to little clubs to big stadiums, back to little clubs, and get people to like this. And going through the struggle of when people was disrespecting and you still deal with them to make this culture really happen from country to country. My thing was to break doors down and make it where others could just go in and feel happy and play and make that money."

AFRIKA BAMBAATAA WAS THE FIRST B-boy bohemian icon the hiphop world had ever known.

Riding the 26 or 30 bus down the Bronx's Allerton Avenue or Boston Road circa the mid-eighties, I passed time listening to my Walkman (a relatively new experience in itself). I can recollect some of my favorite homemade Maxell XLII-S cassettes: Run-D.M.C.'s *Raising Hell* on side A, Sting's *The Dream of the Blue Turtles* on side B. LL Cool J's *Bigger and Deffer* on side A, David Bowie's *Never Let Me Down* on side B. I felt clever mixing up genres; I personally wasn't surrounded by many cultural mulattoes, author Trey Ellis's term for those of us who glean as much from the over-riding white culture as from our own. Hiphop and Prince were the two dominant artistic forces of my adolescence. Rap music samples led me to seek out James Brown and George Clinton. Prince turned me onto Joni Mitchell, the Beatles, Santana, Jimi Hendrix—much of which I found handy in my parents' collection. Needless to say, *The Hissing of Summer Lawns* was not too popular in my northeast Bronx neighborhood. Critic Nelson George has defined the boho (concerning black folk) as "a thoughtful, self-conscious figure like *A Different World*'s Cree Summer or Living Colour's Vernon Reid, whose range of interest and taste challenges both black and white stereotypes of African-American behavior." Years prior to his definition, I prided myself on embodying the B-boy bohemian. (Fuck labels, naturally—but if you're going to be a monkey you may as well be a gorilla.) Afrika Bambaataa was the very first.

Do you want more? Common. Erykah Badu. André 3000. Mos Def. Q-Tip. ?uestlove of the Roots. De La Soul. The Native Tongues in general, in fact. Lauryn Hill. DJ Spooky. Cee-Lo. Saul Williams. Pharrell Williams and N.E.R.D. Goldie. Digable Planets and Wyclef Jean. Del tha Funkeé Homosapien and Justin Warfield. Prince Paul and John Forté. P. M. Dawn and Basehead. Tricky. Finding hiphoppers equally fluent in both *Mama Said* (Lenny Kravitz) and *Mama Said Knock You Out* (LL Cool J) is not as rare nowadays. Imagine, though, DJ Afrika Bambaataa at the Bronx River center in 1973 sporting a freshly cut mohawk and spinning Aerosmith, Foghat, and the Rolling Stones for a black and Latino crowd. More so than either Grandmaster Flash or Kool DJ Herc, Afrika Bambaataa cuts a rather eccentric figure.

What possessed the young man, gave him the courage? "Well, basically, 'cause I really didn't give a shit and I knew I had an army behind me, so you could bring it on," he says, laughing. "A lot of other DJs had to wait to see if . . . You know, we started playing 'Honky Tonk Women' by the Rolling Stones, they waited to see if my audience would respond and take it. [Then] they tried it on they thing and it worked. That's what made the basis of hiphop music or the break music, the Zulu Nation records that we brought out that many still use to this day."

The interracial bands and multicultural outlook of the Jimi Hendrix Experience and especially Sly & the Family Stone were fresh on Afrika Bambaataa's mind as well. Often compared with late jazz bandleader Sun Ra as a cult figure, he is quick to clarify: "I knew Sun Ra music from the jazz day but what influenced me is Sly & the Family Stone completely. It was the first interracial band breaking down barriers. Dealing with racism: 'Don't Call Me Nigger, Whitey.' Back on they *Dance to the Music* album they had a cut where they was rapping."

RAP AS A PROFIT-GENERATING ENGINE is often powered by the fuel of its lowest common denominator: providing violent, escapist ghetto fantasy to a hugely white, suburban, teenage consumer base. Nothing succeeds quite like black spectacle where Americana is concerned, from the legends of Stagger Lee and John Henry right up to the shot, stabbed, and jailed extravaganza of the nouveau riche 50 Cent. The multinational corporations responsible for packaging, distributing, and promoting rap music worldwide have no true interest in the welfare of the community that invented and produced hiphop culture, really. Such is the nature of capitalism and racist exploitation. It behooves such a power structure, obviously, to assume the onus of defining the commodity of hiphop in order to box it up and sell it back to those who created it, as well as to those higher on the socioeconomic plane with deeper pockets. But I posit that if anyone has an inherent right to define what hiphop is or isn't, it's Afrika Bambaataa.

According to Afrika Bambaataa, hiphop has a fifth element. Modern dictionaries (alongside definitions of *dis* and *bling-bling*) define hiphop as a teenage subculture including emceeing, deejaying, breaking, and graf—the classic four elements. If you've seen the Pillsbury Doughboy rhyme or Barney Rubble backspin for his Fruity Pebbles then you already know this. The fifth element of hiphop cannot be marketed to fatten company coffers, nor would it benefit big businesses that pimp the culture to popularize this element.

The fifth element of hiphop is knowledge.

You are not to blame if you have never heard of the Infinity Lessons, though you owe yourself a visit to Zulunation.com if you haven't. "As we progressed on into the eighties we started adding the Infinity Lessons dealing with knowledge," Afrika Bambaataa says. "We say in the Zulu Nation that knowledge is infinite. You seek knowledge from the cradle to the grave." A positivist, metaphysical vibe permeates the Infinity Lessons along with the influence of spiritual leaders like the Nation of Islam's Elijah Muhammad and Dr. Malaki York of Ansaru Allah. The Infinity Lessons speak to issues of health ("Before you try modern medicine, try the herbal cure for your everyday problems"), success ("The most potent force is positive thinking"), independent thinking ("We as Zulus of all races, colors, and creeds should study research on everything that's anything and should always be thinking people and not zombies. It is our duty as Zulus and human beings to search for truth and nothing but truth"), and the power of the mind. Infinity Lessons on mind power recall the teachings of early twentieth century texts like Prentice Mulford's *Thought Forces* and *The Science of Mind* by Ernest Holmes. (An excerpted Infinity Lesson: "The mind is the supreme force and power. It is above all matter. The mind is living energy, knowledge is potential energy, and when in activation it becomes living energy.") Afrika Bambaataa says that when creating the Zulu Nation he "was already in conscious teachings of the Honorable Elijah Muhammad, Dr. Malaki Z. York and the Ansaru Allah community, Young Lords, and the Black Panther Party. A little bit after the Black Spades I became a member of the Nation of Islam, after I left the Five Percent Nation."

This is hiphop, above and beyond the bare booties and trappings of materialism force-fed to the public on music television. Headed out of our meeting at the National Black Theatre, Afrika Bambaataa advises to "take hiphop culture back into the peace, unity, love, and having fun. Stop all this gossiping and negative talk against each other and get a hiphop unity foundation where we police ourself, get health benefits for ourselves, and health insurance. And like York and them say, we want right knowledge, right wisdom, right overstanding, and right sound reasoning."

Spouting practices that sound similar to the right thinking, right mindfulness, right view, etc. of Buddhism's noble eightfold path, Afrika Bambaataa enters a black SUV and is swiftly driven off to the Bronx.

Notes Toward a Hiphop Politik

RUSSELL SIMMONS, known for decades as Rush to his close friends, is of average height and build for a man his age (forty-six), with a clean-shaven face, bald dome, and light complexion. In conversation, he is likely to switch gears from hiphop culture and Eastern spirituality to politics and rap-industry commerce several times in the span of ten minutes. He was born in Jamaica, Queens, the son of Howard University graduates, and moved to residential Hollis at eight; dealt marijuana and was very briefly warlord of the seventeenth division of the Seven Immortals gang during the 1970s; and eventually attended, then dropped out of, City College a few credits short of a sociology degree.

In the halcyon days of hiphop, Simmons managed the seminal rap acts Kurtis Blow, Whodini, and Run-D.M.C. (his younger brother is Joseph "Run" Simmons, now a reverend) through Rush Management. Shortly thereafter, he founded Def Jam Recordings out of partner Rick Rubin's New York University dorm room, introducing the likes of LL Cool J, the Beastie Boys, and Public Enemy to Middle America. His wildly successful clothing line Phat Farm has been in operation since 1992. He is universally regarded as having established the blueprint of the hiphop multimedia mogul. Russell Simmons *is* hiphop.

Or is he? "Russell, as quiet as it's been kept, you are not hiphop!" begins an open letter circulating on the Internet by rap activist Rosa Clemente—founder of Know Thy Self Productions, a speakers' bureau dedicated to social change and organization of the hiphop generation. "Where were you when the hiphop community united over the issue of AIDS, apartheid, police brutality, gun violence, and the bombing of Vieques, Puerto Rico?" she asks. "You were having those fundraisers for Senator Hillary Clinton, former President Bill Clinton, and having your summer Hampton parties hobnobbing with the likes of Donald Trump and Martha Stewart."

Ask Russell Simmons about Rosa Clemente, and he'll ponder meditatively and then respond sincerely with, "Why do I know her?"

Not long ago I spent some time with Simmons down in mid-Manhattan at the offices of Phat Farm, from where he now operates. We sit in his spacious forty-third-floor office, which is distinguished by a wall-to-wall oriental rug, lots of mahogany wood grain, and gold: gold scales, gold lamps, gold clocks. Magazines adorn various surfaces: *Black Enterprise*; *XXL* featuring popular Def Jam artist Jay-Z on the cover; Russell Simmons's own *Oneworld*. The bookshelf features titles like former mayoral candidate Mark Green's *Selling Out*, and Simmons's own memoir, *Life and Def.* So widely known for conducting business on the move that Motorola recently partnered with him to produce the i90c limited-edition mobile phone, it's slightly strange to see him sitting behind a desk, a candle serenely flickering on the surface next to flowers sprouting from a Phat Farm shoebox.

Speaking with Russell Simmons is, I imagine, akin to taking an audience with the President. We are interrupted several times by various assistants and speakerphone intrusions as we discuss his political leanings of late. Partially responsible for bringing Public Enemy (the revolutionary rap trio that produced the masterpiece of the genre, *It Takes a Nation of Millions to Hold Us Back*) to the world, Simmons has felt the pang of social responsibility since becoming a yoga adherent, marrying wife Kimora Lee, and fathering two children. He spearheaded the creation of the Hiphop Summit Action Network in July 2001—a "coalition of hiphop artists, record company executives, civil rights leaders, [and] community activists," according to its executive director, former NAACP head Dr. Benjamin Chavis—and has been voicing his political opinions like a seasoned pundit. Ask him what sparked his greater awareness, and his answer is characteristically two parts reflection, one part filibuster.

"They ask this question all the time. I'm never really satisfied with my answer," he starts. "But it's a little bit of a greater connection with myself. It started seven, eight years ago with yoga practice. I started reading all the propaganda, the yoga sutras and the basic books, right? Reading that kind of crap. Meditation and the whole physical and spiritual practice has helped though. It gave me a better understanding of my purpose. You know what yoga means, first, right?"

No, I admit.

"'Union with God' is what yoga means. And living in a state of yoga is a state of union with God, which is, like, samadhi. That's what a state of yoga is. That's what you're moving towards, so you know that that's your purpose. And so that is the reason that I'm involved in more social and political stuff. I have my own Foundation for Ethnic Understanding. I have my own Rush Philanthropic Arts Foundation, my own other charitable kind of philanthropic work, all those things, because I have a better relationship with myself, with my higher self."

OF COURSE, POLITICAL MOVEMENTS HAVE BEEN BUILT on spiritual foundations before—think of Mohandas Gandhi, Dr. Martin Luther King Jr., Malcolm X. In keeping with the familiar spiritual axiom that character assessment be based on deeds rather than rhetoric, a fifty-three-year-old, bespectacled Benjamin Chavis enters from his office down the hall to discuss the organization's progress. Simmons takes one of his many persistent phone calls.

"Prior to June 4th, Mayor Bloomberg announced that he was cutting three hundred million dollars additional from the school budget. This was on top of the four hundred million dollars that Giuliani had made the year before," says Chavis. "Nine days before June 4th, Russell and the Hiphop Summit Action Network called for young people to come after school, to meet us down at the City Hall. The teachers, who had already planned a rally that day, were planning for maybe ten thousand people. Well, one hundred thousand young people showed up, and it was unprecedented.

"It was the largest urban mobilization," he continues, "and it was not only that Jay-Z, P. Diddy, LL Cool J, Doug E. Fresh, Alicia Keys, Erykah Badu, and Rah Digga came to speak, but they spoke on the issue. They were clear that we want an equal, quality education, that we were protesting these budget cuts. The next day, the mayor restored two hundred ninety-eight million dollars back into the budget. So that was a tremendous victory. And it showed that we have the ability to flex a certain muscle in terms of mobilization."

Benjamin Chavis exits, but he is far from the final visitor to Simmons's office. Simmons mentions that the celebrated yoga instructor Sharon Gannon attended his 2000 fundraiser for Hillary Clinton, and soon someone enters with a copy of her book *The Art of Yoga.* ("You can have it. It's a beautiful book," he says.) Two middle-aged white men breeze through to pitch a high-energy beverage for hiphop consumption that will become Def-Con 3. Gary Foster, who works closely with Simmons on the Hiphop Summit Action Network, is introduced at one point, and some discussion of press in the *New York Times* takes place. Simmons is constantly hustling, hence the nickname Rush. One man's hustler, however, is another man's politician, and at times, Simmons seems poised for his own mayoral bid. He looks me squarely in the eye and vehemently denies any interest in political office, not the first time he's done so. "I have no aspirations. To move young people to a higher consciousness is my greatest aspiration, to make a difference in terms of young people."

IN THE JUNE 2002 ISSUE OF *The Source*—the largest selling music magazine on nationwide newsstands—Russell Simmons and Benjamin Chavis published "Power Movement," an essay detailing a fifteen-point agenda for the Hiphop Summit Action Network. (Until recently, the organization's headquarters were at *The Source*.) The "social, political, and economic development and empowerment of our families and communities" ranks highest; environmental concerns also rate, as Point Fifteen protests the targeting of low-income communities for toxic waste dumps and other environmentally hazardous developments. Point Nine states, "We want reparations to help repair the lingering vestiges, damages, and suffering of African Americans as a result of the brutal enslavement of generations of Africans in America." The reparations issue is serious to him, and it serves to highlight the synergy a man as enterprising as Russell Simmons is able to generate for his causes.

The Phat Farm Classic, a sneaker that enjoyed unprecedented success in 2002 ("We sold two million"), was buoyed by a campaign promoting awareness for reparations featuring Run of Run-D.M.C. "I have 'reparations rallies,' quote unquote, or sneaker parties all over the country," says Russell

Simmons. "And I do interviews on every radio station and morning show as I get to each city, and we talk about the reparations movement." Money contributed to the reparations cause is admittedly minimal, he says. But countering suspicions that he's out to sell sneakers under the guise of a political issue, he opines, "It's really about awareness. We just gave fifteen million dollars to the [Millions for Reparations] March. I don't believe it's a racial issue. I think it's a simple American justice issue. Reparations is greater affirmative action. It's underwriting better job training in communities where it's necessary, or equal high-quality education. It's a way of repairing the past. Repairing the past is a simple meaning of reparations, right? Repairing the past is giving opportunity, access to America. And the government owes us access, greater access. We just want to increase dialogue."

A HIPHOP POLITICAL MOVEMENT may sound curious to those with only a peripheral understanding of the culture and its goings-on. Though materialistic, nihilistic, often misogynistic rappers like 50 Cent and Jay-Z command the attention of mainstream record buyers and video networks, hiphop has an active social consciousness. MCs like Lauryn Hill, Blackalicious, Mos Def, dead prez, and numerous others provide balance to the oft-popularized nihilistic arm. Politicizing the hiphop nation is not necessarily the greatest challenge facing the efforts of the Hiphop Summit Action Network; that's already happened, to some extent anyway. More to the point is that preexisting grassroots hiphop activists are bound to take issue with the network as a come-lately group stealing the media thunder for efforts that have long been underway.

"Malcolm X Grassroots Movement, Youth Force, Youth Ministries for Peace and Justice, Sista 2 Sista, El Puente Youth Academy, Prison Moratorium Project: All those organizations work around issues such as political prisoners, the Rockefeller drug laws, the prison industrial complex, police brutality, violence against women, the AIDS epidemic in our community," Rosa Clemente writes in her open letter to Simmons. "Give me a call and I will help set up the meeting so you can meet them. Instead of hosting one of your many fundraisers for white elected officials, why don't you host a fundraiser or, better yet, attend one of the many events and mobilizations that these black and Latino/a youth organize?"

Traveling to South Bronx High School in a limousine with director Ellen Haddigan and four starring poets of *Def Poetry Jam on Broadway* for some community outreach, Russell Simmons responds calmly to these fiery charges. "I don't know of them," he readily admits. "I'm just meeting them now. I don't know why they call themselves 'hiphop'— they don't know no rappers. But I do know why: They're young, they're from this generation and all that shit. But they don't have any influence, except that they have their heart, and they're hard-working. And they're probably a lot more educated and sophisticated than I am about all the issues that I'm supposed to be involved in that they're involved in. I want to be connected to every one of 'em. And I want them to be connected to us. We'd love that. So, I mean, she's right. I don't know exactly what else she said. What she think, that we're not trying to talk to them?"

Well, maybe more that you are trying to hold out the Hiphop Summit Action Network as the premiere rap activist organization, I suggest.

"I ain't tryin to do shit. I'm tryin to get Jay-Z to be premiere. My job is to get Jay-Z to be the premiere . . . He saw the poetry [on Broadway] last night, he was inspired. I hope he changes. He moves people in all kinds of ways."

THE TENDENCY IS TO CHARACTERIZE MY GENERATION as politically apathetic, disillusioned toward the democratic process. Much is made of the fact that more black men are incarcerated in the prison system than enrolled in institutions of higher learning, more products of the problem than part of any possible solution. As a demographic we have waxed and waned, alternately drawn to the promise of the American dream the nation lays bare and reeling from the hypocrisy of its pungent policies. Reaping the benefits of the civil rights movement as a given, the hiphop generation formed our social consciousness amid a climate of very particular circumstances. The evolution of our awareness travels a number of political stages; a discernible arc of development shines through upon inspection of our unique collective experience.

1. *SCHOOLHOUSE ROCK* AND THE INSIDIOUS THEORY OF MULTICULTURALISM

Kids don't have much of a political sensibility, granted. But one's eventual outlook on the world is certainly born during the single-digit years of action figures, Apple Jacks cereal, coloring books, and Bosco chocolate syrup. Distilling the macrocosm of the hiphop generation experience down to the microcosm of my own personal experience—I can really only speak for myself, and I'm somewhat good at it—the mass media available to a preadolescent in the mid-seventies imparted several decidedly political messages.

Watching television during that era, it failed to dawn on me that all cartoon characters as recent as even a decade prior were Caucasian-colored cathode rays of light. (Except for various sambo caricatures, another topic for another time.) As a child I was never greatly impressed by the *Jackson Five Cartoon* that began airing on ABC in 1971; it was too obvious to my discerning ears that the voices weren't the true J5. Bill Cosby launched *Fat Albert and the Cosby Kids* on CBS in 1972 and the show became a favorite once I graduated from *The Electric Company* (itself featuring a thirty-something Morgan Freeman in Spider-Man skits). This can all be taken for granted now, the realization of King's dream that "little black boys and black girls would be able to join hands with little white boys and white girls as sisters and brothers"; that revolution was a TV-land reality by the time I was teething. The insertion of characters like the bass-playing Valerie in *Josie and the Pussycats* (1970) or Black Vulcan, Samurai, and Apache Chief in *The All-New Super Friends Hour* (1977) conveyed the harmony of a multicultural, multiethnic America to a legion of black children who were legally prohibited from peeing in the same toilet as white children in the South before the 1954 *Brown vs. the Board of Education* verdict.

Which brings us to *Schoolhouse Rock* and "The Great American Melting Pot." A venerable staple of Generation X/hiphop generation childhood, *Schoolhouse Rock* premiered on ABC in 1973 as the network's solution to parental and political criticism over its violent Saturday morning television programming. This entertaining and educational series of animated cartoon shorts starring children of every stripe and hue is warmly familiar to almost anyone who was a youth during that era. The first song on De La Soul's classic *3 Feet High and Rising* is "The Magic Number," a song musically structured around "Three Is a Magic Number," a cartoon devised to teach multiplication tables. And when Atlantic Records released *Schoolhouse Rock Rocks* in the mid-nineties, beatbox pioneer Biz Markie speak-sang his way through "The Energy Blues"—a tune/cartoon about the environmental consequences of irresponsible energy consumption. *Schoolhouse Rock* lessons on math, science, grammar, and history helped many a kid through elementary school exams.

Great American Melting Pot
Ingredients: Armenians, Africans, English, Dutch, Italians, Chinese, Poles, Irish, Germans, Puerto Ricans, Portuguese, Spanish, Swedes, Norwegians, Russians, Greeks, Cubans, Mexicans

In "The Great American Melting Pot," from the "America Rock" bundle of history cartoons, lovely Lady Liberty (an animated Statue of Liberty) flips through her book of recipes, settling on the dish above. The insidious inference of cartoon characters of diverse nationalities simmering in a North America–shaped pot is that they blend into an altogether new stew devoid of their original cultures' flavor. "You simply melt right in, it doesn't matter what your skin," goes the song, punctuating a narrative essentially about the migration of European immigrants to the United States. Completely absent from this Old World/New World construction, of course, is any account of the peculiar institution that brought African Americans to these shores, not to mention the omission of Haitians, Jamaicans, Japanese, Dominicans, Indians, Filipinos, Palestinians, Koreans, Pakistanis, Arabs, Trinidadians, Colombians, Guyanese, or Native Americans from the recipe.

My political consciousness (and that of millions of other black children of the time, no doubt) was limited, albeit rather self-hating. The overriding message received from the dominant culture was to morph oneself into a white Anglo-Saxon Protestant. To the mind of a child, slavery and segregation seem like the atrocities of a long-gone age (the miniseries adaptation of Alex Haley's *Roots* aired when

I was a six-year-old and I didn't watch it, having no inter-est in altering my self-image with that graphic historical presentation), and criticism leveled against white folks by one's family sounds mostly like racism. At this stage you buy into the American dream. If you could "melt right in" by changing your name from Lifshitz to Lauren or invest-ing in some choice rhinoplasty, you would. But then there's that pesky melanin problem, Ambi Skin Discoloration Fade Cream for Normal Skin® notwithstanding.

2. THE GOVERNMENT'S RESPONSIBLE: CULTURAL NATIONALISM, REPATRIATION, AND SEPARATISM

The all-inclusive, Technicolor-rainbow "We are the world" of youth turns to black and white around puberty, not coin-cidentally. For me, the mild sting of not being invited to var-ious bar mitzvahs of thirteen-year-old Jewish friends finally underscored some fundamental cultural differences. The Shorehaven Beach Club—a summertime swimming pool popular with Jews in the Soundview section of the Bronx near the East River—held too strong a reputation for dis-crimination for me to accept my friends' invitations to hang out, and few were proffered. But puberty, ultimately the final straw, tips the scale. Rejection by the young girls you're sud-denly smitten by is a dire enough situation without the added doubts of, is it because I'm a black guy? is it because she can't take me home to her parents? Self-consciousness sets in when peer pressure over white friends surfaces, the oreo (black on the outside, white on the inside) jokes begin, interracial sleepovers taper off. And in my specific case, circa 1984, whites just did *not* get hiphop. Anyone who prefers Chicago to the Fat Boys deserves to be excommunicated, immediately.

In short order you find yourself in a scenario straight out

of Dr. Beverly Tatum's *Why Are All the Blacks Sitting Together in the Cafeteria*, pounding out beats on tables as classmates freestyle lyrics or recite from rhyme books. And somehow, someway, the late El-Hajj Malik El-Shabazz makes his way to you. In the hammock summer between my ninth and tenth grades, black cultural nationalism hit hard as many peers became Five Percenters, seeking knowledge of self from teachings of the Nation of Gods and Earths (an offshoot of the Nation of Islam). Though they took issue with his later repudiation of deceased N.O.I. leader Elijah Muhammad, Malcolm X still commanded much respect in Five Percent ciphers where daily lessons were being run down. As friends renounced pork from their diets, absorbing crucial information on blacks being the original people to populate the planet (the four-million-year-old remains of Dinknesh—the oldest excavated bones in history—were found in Ethiopia; what does that tell *you*?), I chose *The Autobiography of Malcolm X* from an elective criminology class reading list.

And Malcolm X, if nothing else, sets off the domino effect. The Black Panthers invoked the Second Amendment to the Constitution and legally, publicly toted shotguns? Marcus Garvey incorporated the Black Star Line to return blacks to Africa? Knowledge touted as originating from Greeks in Alexandria was actually raided Egyptian knowledge? An us/them dynamic begins to assert itself.

Back when a majority of popular rappers were teenagers themselves, more closely mirroring their record-buying constituency, trends in the music more accurately reflected the sentiments of the hiphop republic at large. Like some manifest outgrowth of collective consciousness, MCs in the late 1980s began to demonstrate a political mindset (heretofore unseen save for 1982's "The Message" by Grandmaster Flash and the Furious Five). Rakim revolutionized rap language with 1987's *Paid in Full*, popularizing Five Percenter linguistics. Public Enemy debuted the same year as the "Black Panthers of rap" with *Yo! Bum Rush the Show*; shotgun props were worked into the choreography of PE's onstage visual foil, the S1Ws (Security of the First World). KRS-One's political commentary blossomed on *By All Means Necessary*, the 1988 sophomore album of Boogie Down Productions. This trio inspired other like-minded individuals: Paris, Brand Nubian, Poor Righteous Teachers, X-Clan.

My generation questioned customary Eurocentric cultural style and perspectives, embracing what Dr. Molefi Asante dubbed "Afrocentricity" in his 1990 book of the same name, exemplified by the kente cloth, cowrie shell fashions, and subject matter in the songs of the Jungle Brothers, A Tribe Called Quest, De La Soul, Queen Latifah, Arrested Development, and others. The cumulative effect of AIDS, police brutality, gun violence, crack culture, and eight years of Reaganomics on the black population produced this militant mind state within the young hiphop community, and our music, our voice, spoke to those conditions. (Along with the occasional "Pickin' Boogers"—the tom-tom cries, the tom-tom laughs.)

I chose to apply to the historically black Morehouse College in 1988, the same year their alum Spike Lee released *School Daze* (based at the fictional, historically black Mission College) and NBC began airing *A Different World* (a spin-off of *The Cosby Show* based at the fictional, historically black Hillman College). *A Different World* was canceled during its sixth season in 1993, the year I graduated. Serendipity is an amazing thing. Comedienne T'keyah "Crystal" Keymáh of Fox Television's *In Living Color* variety show invented a character named Crissy for a recurring skit about Black World, a place where everything was "good and black" with no sign of the dominant white culture anywhere around. Given the political sensibility I shared with hiphop peers, adopting the Black World aesthetic as a lifestyle seemed a viable, attractive option. After graduating from an African-American institution, the most significant jobs of my professional career included positions at the fanzine *Black Beat*, *XXL*, the urban-culture mag *Vibe*, and the website of BET during the dotcom boom. Ironically, all those media outlets were white-owned: by Sterling/MacFadden Partnership, Harris Publications, Miller Publishing Group, and Viacom, respectively.

3. "DEMOCRACY IS THE WORST SYSTEM DEVISED BY THE WIT OF MAN, EXCEPT FOR ALL THE OTHERS."
—WINSTON CHURCHILL

Predictably, the black and white vantage turns a murky gray with maturity. The most radical answers to the so-called Negro Question begin to reveal logistical holes upon scrutiny. Repatriation to Africa is not out of the question; I have friends who relocated to Ghana and South Africa as young adults. But needless to say, the vast European colonization of the nineteenth and twentieth centuries transformed the continent immensely from my generation's idealized notions of the Motherland, if indeed those utopian notions ever bore any actual resemblance to Africa. Blacks established the foundation of the American economy with over a century of forced, free labor. To abandon a nation we helped build no longer seems the wisest move. Our families were decimated once already through institutionalized slavery; the reality of deserting parents, grandparents, uncles, aunts, and cousins for the faraway shores of Africa, to say nothing of the abandonment of our struggling communities here in America, largely loses its appeal into our twenties. Separatism fails as well, whether idealized (see the above limitations of Black World) or actual (seceding from the United

States and receiving an apportionment of our own land from the government—once endorsed as a goal by the Nation of Islam—is a clear and obvious impossibility).

Hiphop excelled politically at problem-identification in the late eighties but came up short at problem-solving come the early nineties. Maybe the complications of brainstorming solutions created the stone wall politically conscious hiphop collided into. Hiphop's critique of the establishment dwindled as the community was released from a twelve-year Republican chokehold; celebration of capitalism and entrepreneurship increased during the Clinton administration. In the 1990s young rap record-label CEOs like Bad Boy Entertainment's Sean Combs and Roc-a-Fella Records' Damon Dash became as central to establishing the paradigm of materialism in rap as Public Enemy and KRS-One had been to political consciousness.

Sixties civil rights activists were brutalized by police dogs, fire-hosed, jailed, and sometimes killed to win the right to the ballot. As the attempt to mobilize hiphop into a political bloc began—by Russell Simmons with the Hiphop Summit Action Network as well as self-professed "hiphop minister" Conrad Muhammad with his organization, Conscious Hiphop Activism for Global Empowerment (CHHANGE)—the first major actions involved mass voter registration. The militant defenses of my generation against joining "the system" were lowered by historical examples like former Black Panther Bobby Rush's 1992 appointment to the House of Representatives and the two high-profile presidential runs of the Reverend Jesse Jackson (stamped by a hiphop seal of approval from Grandmaster Melle Mel on 1984's "Jesse").

"I believe that as African Americans we can be critical of this country but we have to embrace our American-ness and we have to embrace the process," Conrad Muhammad told a *New York Press* reporter in 2002. "I've really grown to believe that we have the best political system in the world. I've grown to appreciate democracy. You may not like the way things are but you have a right to say it and in a lot of countries you don't." Conrad Muhammad—former head minister of the same Harlem mosque previously led by Malcolm X and Minister Louis Farrakhan—parted from the Nation of Islam in 1998 and formed CHHANGE to tap the political potential of the hiphop generation. In a contentious, eyebrow-raising move, Conrad Muhammad threw in a bid for congressional office in 2002 . . . as a Republican ("Why shouldn't we place ourselves in that party and leverage our influence in both parties?" he questioned), and later returned to Christianity, preaching as Baptist minister Conrad Tillard.

With the maturity of young adulthood one realizes that the black mentality is not so monolithic as to insist upon a single, rigid political approach, and that barring its history of Native American genocide and African-American enslavement, democracy comes closer to a fair, just system of governance for modern society than any other existing system. At this stage—with a wiser, more skeptical eye—you once again believe in the American dream.

4. NEW WORLD ORDER: "PRESIDENT" GEORGE W. BUSH AND SEPTEMBER 11

Funny how those stages involving a belief in the American dream are always associated with no small dose of naïveté. The Joint Center for Political and Economic Studies announced a total of 9,040 black elected officials nationwide in 2000, an all-time high. Yet despite over forty years of civil rights–enabled political appointments, a study conducted by economists David Clingaman, Richard Vedder, and Lowell Gallaway reported that the average income for a black

American is annually 61 percent lower than the average white income, the same percentage difference as existed in 1880. As well, black unemployment levels have remained approximately twice that of whites since 1954. The 2000 Census lists African Americans as 12 percent of the U.S. population, yet we make up 49 percent of the prison population, incarcerated at a rate over nine-and-a-half times higher than that of whites due to disparities in the criminal justice system like New York's Rockefeller drug laws and Proposition 205—the "three strikes" law—in California.

Hiphop has aged enough to encompass more than one generation: both so-called Generation X (born from 1964–1977) and Generation Y (1977–1995), if you will. While the above information may move both factions of hiphop to anger, rap's new generation may be more invigorated to do something about it (egged on by a new political wave of MCs: Common, Ms. Dynamite, Talib Kweli, the Coup, Zion I). Entering into the 2000s, many my age began to prioritize home ownership, climbing corporate ladders, providing for our children, and maintaining marital relationships over "the struggle" and "nation building." And granted, the personal is political—it is of vast import that strong black families are maintained and that hiphop is able to establish a debt-free, financially healthy foundation. But this final stage in the arc of political consciousness for my age group reveals a lethargy that overcomes even that of the dominant American population.

Only 51 percent of the eligible voting population cast ballots for the 2000 presidential election—around 100,000,000 of a potential 281,427,000—including approximately 10,000,000 blacks. (Disenfranchised from voting due to past incarceration are about 1,460,000 black men who nevertheless file annually with the Internal Revenue Service, taxation without representation—". . . and that's not fair!" says

Schoolhouse Rock's "No More Kings.") The black voter is often galvanized to elect the candidate who stands for the lesser of two evils; the hiphop voter has no true representative speaking for such Hiphop Summit Action Network agenda issues as reparations or universal health care, and so voting devolves into a perfunctory exercise. As a result of this mentality, the spoils of votes go to politicians who best represent certain key issues without actually doing anything about them once elected, often ultimately reversing their positions altogether.

Certainly nothing in recent history has done more to encourage voter apathy than the 2000 election of President George W. Bush. As a matter of public record, former Vice-President Al Gore actually won the popular vote of that election, receiving 539,898 more votes than Bush. The outcome of the election boiled down to a recount of votes in Florida (a state represented by governor Jeb Bush, George W.'s brother). Thousands of eligible black voters were prohibited from casting votes on election day, as Database Technologies removed 173,000 registered voters from Florida's voter rolls on the suspicion that they might be former felons. An additional eight thousand names were struck from the rolls—including felons whose voting privileges had been reinstated, as well as citizens who had only committed misdemeanors like littering and parking violations—due to Database's reliance on a false list supplied by the state of Texas, where George W. Bush served as governor. Hundreds of black Floridians qualified to exercise their Constitutional right to vote were turned away at the polls; Bush was officially credited with 537 more votes than Al Gore following the recount.

Members of the civil rights generation all recall where they were when President John F. Kennedy, Malcolm X, and Dr. Martin Luther King Jr. were assassinated. Often equated with those pivotal historical moments is my generation's loss of rappers Tupac Shakur and Christopher Wallace a/k/a the Notorious B.I.G., and I do indeed remember my where-abouts at the time of their murders. But four years following the death of B.I.G., hiphop received an even greater genera-tional benchmark.

I woke up that Tuesday morning sometime after ten A.M. having ignored the ringing telephone; three messages from my mother and an ex-girlfriend blinked on my answering machine. I logged onto the Internet from my Brooklyn apartment to check email and was greeted by an America Online pop-up. Two airplanes had collided into the World Trade Center downtown; the buildings were in flames. (Bear in mind, flaming Twin Towers were depicted on the cover of Jeru the Damaja's 1994 *The Sun Rises in the East,* as well as the scheduled-for-November 2001 *Party Music* by the Coup.) I received an Instant Message from an editor cancel-ing our weekly meeting and suggesting I turn on my televi-sion. As I tuned in, the towers fell. Black smoke billowed in the sky outside my Brooklyn apartment.

We are not stupid, the population of my generation. As a result of our distrust of American society, many of us have been prone to absorbing conspiracy-laced tomes like William Cooper's popular 1991 *Behold a Pale Horse.* Members of Mobb Deep and Wu-Tang Clan subscribed religiously to its revelations of the impending "Illuminati" and New World Order of biological bar-code and microchip implants as the millennium approached. But truth is evermore stranger than fiction, and the monumental events of September 11, 2001 have inspired more individual research into the state of world affairs and America's standing in the international arena than any other incident in hiphop history.

The politically conscious among us wholly rejected President Bush's fabrications about Osama bin Laden's motivating hate for secularism, capitalism, democracy, and individualism. We, more than any other group, are used to the government lying to us. We have investigated on our own. The Internet (invented by the Pentagon, ironically enough) is an amazing technology. No need for conspiracy theories: It is incontrovertible knowledge that America is the only nation condemned by the World Court of the United Nations for international terrorism in 1986, for the death of tens of thousands in Nicaragua. (The U.S. was ordered to terminate their unlawful use of force and pay substantial reparations; it did neither, dismissing the court's judgment.) It is uncontestable that Osama bin Laden belongs to a cadre of about 100,000 radical Islamist extremists trained by the CIA to do war with Russian invaders of Afghanistan in the 1970s, and that this network subsequently took on an agenda of its own to assassinate President Anwar Sadat of Egypt in 1981, and even ousted American military forces in Lebanon in 1983. The least educated of the hiphop community know that war against Iraq is rooted in economic interests revolving around oil.

We are not stupid, despite how we are portrayed in music videos disseminated by the record companies of multinational corporations. As our tax dollars go to providing bullets and bombs for the slaughter of innocents in Iraq while resistance seems futile, know that we are concocting new strategies for countering what cultural critic bell hooks calls imperialist white-supremacist capitalist patriarchy.

YOU CAN HEAR A PIN DROP. My eyes are shut and my mind is wandering, though it's not supposed to be. An orange tabby brushes past. I'm sitting in lotus position on a pillow in the living room of a woman I met fifteen minutes ago, shortly after eleven A.M. on a Saturday morning. Six strangers—two men, four women, all white—meditating, surround me. This is a peace circle.

An hour ago I exited my garden (read: basement) apartment in tony Clinton Hill for the even tonier Brooklyn neighborhood of Park Slope, *lets get free* by dead prez pealing from headphones as I patiently awaited Duke Ellington's famed A train and then transferred to the F. Throughout March 2002 I engaged in an email correspondence with Mary Myers, spiritual activist and leader of the borough's only peace circle; Manhattan boasts two peace circles with one convening biweekly on Staten Island; hundreds exist worldwide. She invited me to attend a meeting and I acquiesced, with nearly no idea what to expect.

How did I find out about peace circles? The story starts with author Neale Donald Walsch and *Conversations with God*, a late-nineties trilogy of new-agey spiritual volumes so popular that they sold in excess of two-and-a-half million copies—*Book One* remained on the *New York Times* Bestseller List for fifty-six weeks. I read them all fairly fast, entertained by Walsch's dialogue with the God of his conscience, examining money, love, evil, sex, health, diet, and relationship issues. My mother—an open-minded but nevertheless God-revering Christian—borrowed a book or two after Walsch's inevitable appearance on the *Oprah Winfrey Show*. She enjoyed it, but advised her firstborn against supporting or donating money to any organization that might appear listed at the back of the books, leery of any potential cult connections. Still, it's rare that I read any nonfiction book and agree with 98 percent of what I come across, especially concerning matters of the spirit. So, like a hardheaded kid, I combed through the afterword of *Book Three* and discovered the Global Renaissance Alliance.

Time out. I recognize this is an aside within an aside. But it bears mentioning that hiphop culture has no beef with the new-age movement, traditionally tagged occultist (at worst) and touchy-feely (at best). As recent as December 2002 Common released a song about the Aquarian age, and way back in 1997 stalwart MC KRS-One—no hippie rapper, with songs like "9mm Goes Bang" to his credit—rhymed lines like:

> *Truth is truth, whether or not you like me*
> *We are living now in the age of Pisces*
> *But Pisces is over at the year 2000*
> *When the sun of God changes his House and*
> *Enters the age of Aquarius*

And followed a stanza later with:

> *It's called the age of Aquarius*
> *When logic and truth will take care of us*
> *So in this age of spiritual dignity*
> *You'll see a rise in femininity and creativity*
> *Meshed with masculinity, you got to get with me*

Many of the hiphop generation who lived through the culture's Afrocentric phase took that period's faddish fixation to a deeper level. During my time at Morehouse College, with so many pledging Greek-letter fraternities, a few students founded KMT ASEN (an organization named for Old Kingdom–period Egypt) and studied ancient Kemetic history, philosophy, and science. The trappings of this education can be found in the style of hiphop singer Erykah Badu (the record producer of Common's "Aquarius" who is well aware of the Kemetic foundation of astrology). With the late twentieth century mainstreaming of spirituality—recall the short-lived talk show and brisk book sales of Yoruba priest-ess/holistic practitioner Iyanla Vanzant; the unprecedented publishing success of the spiritual-leaning *O, the Oprah Magazine*; the Middle America readership enjoyed by meta-physician Deepak Chopra—it should come as no surprise that a sizable portion of the hiphop community meditates, eats vegetarian, and embraces left-of-center spiritual values.

But I digress. "[T]he Alliance actively proclaims a vision of an America delivered from the clutches of greed, grounded in peace, and evolving toward even more love," writes Marianne Williamson, cofounder with Neale Donald Walsch of the Global Renaissance Alliance (est. 1998). "The [GRA] is not a traditionally issue-oriented political organization." The love movement is bound to sound like a rather soft agenda, I admit. Reconciled with some of the late speeches of Dr. Martin Luther King Jr., however, I'm not so sure. ("When I speak of love I am not speaking of some sentimental and weak response," King said in 1967. "I am speaking of that force which all of the great religions have seen as the supreme unifying principle of life. Love is somehow the key that unlocks the door which leads to ultimate reality.") King's focus on love as the fundamental principle guiding the universal struggle for freedom, as well as the nonviolent code articulated and advanced by Mohandas Gandhi, is the basis for the spiritual politics of the Global Renaissance Alliance. Curious enough to want to see spiritual activism in practice, I accessed the GRA website (Renaissancealliance.org) that explained the concept of the peace circle and listed contact information for like-minded individuals hosting such circles nationwide, even in Brooklyn.

I AM THE FIRST TO ARRIVE, shutting off my dead prez CD in the Park Slope apartment of Mary Myers, a Buddhist in her thirties with a generous amount of spiritualist authors in her library (Thich Nhat Hanh, Thomas Merton, Pema

Chodron, Sharon Salzberg, Bernie Glassman, Charlotte Joko Beck). Regulars begin to file in as we make small talk by her studio grand piano: Rico from San Francisco; a guy named Gili from the Washington, D.C. area; and Millicent, a quite fetching blonde from Ireland. Millicent is hosting next week's peace circle and I make a mental note to show up. Two older women (fifties, maybe) turn up—Sue and Jocelyn—all the way from Long Island. Lord Byron, the orange tabby, slinks between the seven of us conversing over hot tea and bagels.

We begin. Mary Myers makes up a nonsectarian prayer on the spot as we lower heads and close eyes; then she recites, "We bow before the spirit within and receive into our hearts our sister Millicent." Amen to that, I think. Millicent responds in kind to Rico at her left ("This spiritual weaving establishes a sacred circle among the members of the group," suggests Marianne Williamson), and we continue until everyone is acknowledged. Then, for twenty minutes, we silently meditate. Thoughts parade past my mind as I try my best not to dwell on them. I think, government policies and legislation are not the only way to affect change. I think, individuals need to strengthen themselves individually before mobilizing political group efforts. I think, everything is political, every daily life choice: from reducing suffering in the world through a vegetarian diet to not patronizing the "everybody in khakis" globalization efforts of The Gap/Starbucks/McDonald's, to rejecting dominant beauty myths by not straightening one's hair (if one is, say, a female African American). I think, Millicent's blouse is pretty form-fitting.

A flute sounds. Mary Myers brings us out of our relaxed reverie and passes the Native American–carved instrument around as a talking stick from African culture; we take turns holding the floor to describe our vision for the world we would like to inhabit. Eventually the talking stick is passed to me, the only manifestation of hiphop present in the room. I take a controlled breath—inhale, exhale—and my clear mind can think of no more appropriate way to articulate spiritual revolution than to quote Gandhi: "We must be the change we wish to see in the world."

SPELMO BABIES AND OTHER BOURGEOIS EPHEMERA

1.

BLACK WOMEN, GROWN BLACK WOMEN, jump double-dutch on the grass—tresses bouncing, some sneakered, some barefoot, reciting rhymes together as they leap into the swinging ropes. Rick James croons from inside the colonial; black men sit on the veranda eating barbeque from paper plates, sipping on strong mixed drinks under the sunshine. In the distance beautiful young beachgoers relax at the shore, dressed in swimwear and consorting with friends and flirtatious suitors driving convertibles and SUVs up and down Seaview Avenue in the late afternoon. The loudest car stereo system blares Boogie Down Productions' *Criminal Minded*; seagulls fly overhead. The ladies jumping double-dutch call six different states home yet they easily fall into step with the same culturally distinct rhymes from girlhood, skipping through the synchronized swinging ropes, laughing. I had arrived hours ago, parking my Chevy across the water in Cape Cod and catching the forty-five-minute ferry ride to Oak Bluffs. From there a taxi delivered me to the Ink Well, the stretch of sand extending along Nantucket Sound where I'd arranged to meet my law school classmate Hector. He wasn't hard to find despite the hundred other young black revelers laid out on beach towels, socializing, networking, drinking, smoking, swimming, and enjoying the summertime sun. The beach is abuzz with news of *The Source* publisher David Mays's party tonight. Hector leads me to the colonial his friends rented for the week, vacationing urban professionals grilling in the backyard, eye-catching females jumping rope on the lawn. Seating myself inside on a wooden piano bench I start to play Doug E. Fresh and the Get Fresh Crew's "Play This Only at Night" on the upright; it needs tuning. "We figured somebody would show up who knew how to play that thing eventually," says a lovely stranger walking toward the kitchen. Today is Independence Day on Martha's Vineyard.

A popular haven for affluent blacks since the 1890s, Martha's Vineyard island attracts the largely twenty-something progeny of moneyed African-American families during the Fourth of July and Labor Day holidays. Author Lawrence Otis Graham says in *Our Kind of People: Inside America's Black Upper Class,*

> Unlike my brother, I already knew there was *us* and there was *them*. There were those children who belonged to Jack & Jill and summered in Sag Harbor; Highland Beach; or Oak Bluffs, Martha's Vineyard; and there were those who didn't. There were those who graduated from Spelman or Fisk and joined AKA, the Deltas, the Links, and the Girl Friends, and there were those who didn't. There were those fathers who were dentists, lawyers, and physicians from Howard or Meharry and who were Alphas, Kappas, or Omegas and members of the Comus, the Boulé, or the Guardsmen, and there were those who weren't.

Like Graham, I too can lay claim to nearly none of the qualifications above. But the spirit of hiphop is aspirational—according to KRS-One, a part of hiphop's essence is "trying to make a dollar out of fifteen cents"—and I share that spirit on some level, which partially explains my presence at Oak Bluffs.

It is strange to feel like you're "passing" (the infamous practice of light-skinned blacks passing for Caucasians) among your own ethnicity, but socializing with the so-called black elite occasionally engenders that reaction with me; the Bronx Lewises are not steeped in that socially upper-crust society. I accompanied my girlfriend to midtown Manhattan's Copacabana twice as a teenager for the annual Christmastime party sponsored by Jack & Jill (a social organization for the children of black professionals). As a college junior I pledged Alpha Phi Alpha, the oldest black Greek-letter fraternity. I graduated with Bill Cosby's late son Ennis from Morehouse, which Lawrence Otis Graham says is "among the six or seven schools that the old-guard black elite still consider to be most appropriate for their children today." Dating the niece of sportscaster Ahmad Rashad, we drove from the Bronx's Co-op City to her uncle's home in nearby Mount Vernon on Thanksgiving for some family revels, his then wife—*Cosby Show* actress Phylicia Rashad—serving us dessert; one of my more bourgeois moments. But I also know something of free government cheese and Raid roach bombs, which is why socializing with the black bourgeoisie often feels like passing to me.

So the irony of hiphop—voice of the lower socioeconomic class—on Martha's Vineyard is not lost on me, though it doesn't seem to occur to anyone else around me. Ask any layperson to critique hiphop, and the culture's materialistic obsessions will top his or her list of complaints. Driving through Woods Hole in Hector's Continental at nighttime, listening to Nas's *It Was Written* and searching for a party at Hot Tin Roof, it occurs to me that hiphop's notorious materialism bears resemblance to the aspirational elitism surrounding Fourth of July Martha's Vineyard. Elitism equals materialism equals bougieness? Or are they merely related, the roots of one concealed in the others?

2.

VALENTINE'S DAY 1988, I sat in the Whitestone Multiplex transfixed by a meeting of the Gamma Rays (a sorority-type support group to the fictional Gamma Phi Gamma fraternity). The fate of my college matriculation was sealed. All the women were beautiful, I thought, especially actresses Jasmine Guy and Tisha Campbell. I was quite taken at seventeen by Spike Lee's *School Daze*: the football game, the step show, the music, the women (again). The film presented the annual alumni homecoming weekend of the all-black Mission College, exposing the miscellany of issues students encounter: the dynamics between the light-skinned and dark-skinned; between the corporate-bound upwardly mobile and the Afrocentric nationalists; the question of Greek-letter fraternities. Eventually celebrating five home-comings in my own college experience, Spike Lee's vision would prove true to the mark. As I surveyed the alumni weekends at Howard and Morehouse years later in 1994, the symbiotic relationship between elitism, materialism, the bourgeoisie, and young, black hiphop America revealed itself.

Howard University, founded in 1867 to educate newly freed Africans, is located in Washington, D.C. It is the largest historically black school in the country with over eleven thousand students—the majority of whom were probably on hand for the arrival of Nelson Mandela the Friday of that homecoming weekend. I wouldn't know; I am reaching ungodly speeds on the New Jersey Turnpike to arrive in D.C. for the nighttime activities. But this is the type of thing alumni return for: keynote speakers, the football game, parties, and an affirmation of black college camaraderie. Just being a black college alumnus garners me fraternal handshakes and open arms from current and graduated Howard students all weekend. Predominately white universities also celebrate alumni weekends, but a family reunion atmosphere dominates the black college homecoming, and I feel like a cherished cousin.

Dr. Anna Grant, retired chair of Morehouse's sociology department, has seen dozens of homecomings during her thirty-year-plus teaching career. She says historically black colleges and universities "have always had an annual event. During the days of segregation when the places of entertainment, wining, dining, and partying were not open to us, black people created our own venues for entertaining ourselves and having celebrations and reunions. So many of our people have migrated to the North and to the West but they still maintain those family ties, and the extended family has always been a big thing. Black people have always created opportunities to get together and be festive. Bill Cosby talks about the friendship and bonding that goes on at black schools. He says he doesn't have any friends from his undergraduate days at Temple, but that his children's godparents are his wife's [Dr. Camille Cosby, esteemed Howard alumna] college friends. In black schools, we make friends that last a lifetime."

Friday night, cars meet bumper to bumper on Georgia Avenue, the strip running alongside the Howard campus. Just arriving, my friend Jonetta (who briefly attended Atlanta's Morris Brown College), her cousin Alison (a Spelman graduate), and I creep through what feels like an after-hours block party. The Georgia Avenue McDonald's runs out of French fries with so many patrons ordering takeout, crowding the parking lot. Beats by Gang Starr, Jeru the Damaja, and Craig Mack permeate the air from every auto, and Craig Mack is scheduled to perform with a local go-go group on Saturday night. We drive by the African Room but the club scene is dead by two o'clock. The twenty-four-hour International House of Pancakes has the real nightclub vibe, packed to the rim with students eating flapjacks and trading phone numbers. The wait to be seated is half an hour.

On Saturday comes the fashion show. Not the official homecoming fashion show; that was earlier in the week. I mean the multigenerational crowd parading expensive homecoming ensembles in the stands of RFK Stadium, where Howard plays Bethune-Cookman College. After we pass the street team of Bad Boy Entertainment—shirtless record company boosters blowing annoying whistles, circulating promotional CDs, and raising placards that read "THE NEXT GENERATION OF BAD MUTHAFUCKAS"—the game begins. True to *School Daze* (where the Mission football field is never shown), the real game lies in the crowd. Students mill about socializing, rushing back to their seats for the halftime battle of the bands. Young women take care not to drip ketchup on their DKNY, Burberry, AKA, and Delta Sigma Theta jackets. Vendors hawk sorority and fraternity paraphernalia along with T-shirts from Tuskegee, Hampton, Bennett, Lincoln, and other black schools. The Howard Bisons team wins.

The clothes you wear and the car you drive are of immense importance to a large segment of the Howard student population. (The school produced the sartorially splendid millionaire Sean Combs, creator of the Sean John clothing line, who dropped out his freshman year. He famously drives a Bentley.) "Your parents have to be kind of well-off for you to be going there," says Morehouse graduate David Davis, my old schoolmate connection for Prince bootleg tapes. "That's just the crowd that Morehouse and Howard draw—the affluent, top ten percent," he adds, referring to scholar W.E.B. Du Bois's theory that the cream of the black community's talented top ten percent will lead its remainder.

After a couple hours of mixing and mingling outside the football stadium, the masses convene in an armory across the street to watch the Greeks do battle at the homecoming step show. Black fraternities have existed since 1906 when seven students founded Alpha Phi Alpha at Cornell; black sororities started at Howard with Alpha Kappa Alpha in 1908. Students ostensibly pledge to be part of organized community uplift, though many have been known to join for instant social prestige and attention from the opposite sex. Frats and sororities compete by stepping—a combination of boastful raps, choreographed stomps, and handclaps performed a cappella or over music. Tonight Alphas, Sigmas, Omegas, and Kappas as well as AKAs, Deltas, and Zetas all step to Curtis Mayfield's "Freddie's Dead," James Brown's "The Payback," and assorted hiphop, some in Afro wigs no less; there's a seventies theme tonight. Actor Antonio Fargas hosts the stepping competition. As judges deliberate, female R&B trio Y?N-Vee performs, sweatpants sagging seductively low across G-strung asses. The Alphas and AKAs win, then it's off to the next event.

Which happens to be the homecoming concert. Craig Mack may have commanded a standing ovation but I am across town at a more interesting set featuring Method Man, Redman, and the Notorious B.I.G. I think the thirty-dollar cover was a bit steep, as do the roughly fifty other students who bum-rush the door with me. I only catch a few songs from Biggie Smalls, not wanting to leave my less adventurous friends outside too long. Anyway, the main thing for the night, for the weekend, seems to be driving around meeting people and bumping into others you know—then more macking at the pancake house.

THE MOREHOUSE ALUMNI WEEKEND comes around three weeks later. Morehouse's enrollment is smaller than Howard's but the school stands as the biggest and oldest (founded, too, in 1867) college of the Atlanta university center, a Mecca of black education including Spelman and Clark-Atlanta University. My alma mater is the only four-year college for black men in the world, known historically as the black Harvard. By my passenger side for this fourteen-hour road trip is my homeboy Marc; a student at Morris Brown for a few years, he returns "to see the pageantry of the shows. I go for the shows. I like to see who's dancing now, the popular choreographers in the A.U. center. I've choreographed a couple of coronations, pageants, and stuff."

Every Friday on Spelman's campus outside the Manley building, local businesses set up vending booths. Some days, like today, a DJ spins hiphop, and homecoming Friday is always extra festive. (Located across the street from Morehouse's campus, the all-female Spelman College lacks its own homecoming but shares in that of its brother school. So many graduates of Morehouse and Spelman have married one another that a phrase has been coined for their children: spelmo babies. Morehouse graduates Spike Lee and, umm, Farnsworth Bentley are both spelmo babies.)

Redman signs autographs in the crowd, talking up a performance that night with Method Man; actor Allen Payne mills about. In front of Morehouse's Kilgore Center, Black Sheep performs before enthusiastic Morehouse men and rolling BET cameras. Posters tacked to trees around campus announce weekend concerts by the Lady of Rage and Keith Murray. But the talk in the air amid phone numbers being exchanged is of tonight's homecoming coronation at the Martin Luther King Jr. International Chapel. (King is a distinguished Morehouse graduate; so is Gang Starr's Guru.) So after a stop at the Waffle House (where I bump into Atlanta resident Chilli of TLC) I circle back to Morehouse. The coronation band plays tunes by Prince's jazz side-project Madhouse in-between more recognizable R&B instrumentals. Visions of bourgeoisie parade onstage, men dressed in suits and tuxedos accompanying young women wearing ballroom gowns and sequined dresses from the courts of every conceivable Morehouse organization. The crowd *oooh*s and *aaah*s as if anxiously anticipating the day they'll be able to outfit themselves in kind, to attend elite functions and events in the outside world.

"Hell yeah!" says Morehouse grad Spencer Bellamy. "You know that! Some of them can't identify with what's really black. They're, like, lost, and so uppity. I understand that you're about getting ahead but it's all about going ahead and reaching back too, and it seems that they ain't about that. They just got their own cliques and if you ain't driving a nice car or if your parent isn't somebody with dough, some of them people ain't checking for you."

After dinner at Mick's restaurant with a few friends, the next event is the Spelman AKA ball, a dressy affair at a downtown hotel that pretty much embodies Spencer Bellamy's sentiments. AKAs are often typecast as having a prissier image than the other sororities and their event is true to that form. There's fun to be had and beauties galore (plus hiphop in the mix, still) but overall it leaves me wondering what Redman and Method Man are up to.

Homecoming Saturday, Morehouse beats Howard at B. T. Harvey Stadium in a longstanding grudge match that quickens the pulse (especially the Morehouse Tigers cheerleaders). I meet up with more old friends, some of whom toil through graduate schools or law schools like me, and we trade notes and update each other on our lives. The Morehouse-Howard party at the Fox Theatre features more hiphop and more

beauties. Mister Lawnge and Dres of Black Sheep drift aim-
lessly, drinks in their hands.

Suzette Clarke, a Clark-Atlanta graduate floating through
the gathering, offers a counterargument to the question of
certain colleges attracting black elites: "I think black schools
have a little bit of everything that makes up black people.
You got the homeboys and the homegirls, you got the bou-
gies, the black young Republicans, the radical 'kill all the
white people' [types]. People come from all over the world in
the A.U.C. so you're gonna get a mixture of everyone. I don't
think one specific personality prevails. I think it depends on
what clique you're looking at."

3.

REVOLUTION IS IN THE AIR. At a capacity-crowded concert by
De La Soul in downtown Manhattan's Tramps nightclub during 1998, the die is cast. P. Diddy, crowned *Rolling Stone*'s
new king of hiphop less than a year ago, is resoundingly
booed. Lest the irony be lost, when De La Soul released their
3 Feet High and Rising debut in 1989 they were perceived as
flower-power pop purveyors. Afraid of offending grassroots
hiphop listeners with their crossover aspirations, they backed
down from that image and released some of the most quality-
consistent recordings in hiphop (or music in general) in the
process. The golden-age-of-rap trio now commands a sparse
but ardent base of fans, the type eager to topple Sean Combs
from his hippop pedestal. But why, exactly?

"This is true hiphop you listening to right here," rails RZA
on an intro to Wu-Tang Clan's sprawling double album, *Wu-
Tang Forever.* "This ain't no R&B with a wack nigga taking a
loop, relooping that shit, thinking it's gonna be the sound of
the culture. All that player bullshit, dressing up—act like this
some kind of fashion show, man. Fuck that. This is emceeing

right here. This is hiphop." *Wu-Tang Forever* failed to make the hiphop nation safe for democracy (that is, the rap purist's totalitarian state) but at least one message was clear: no more tales of wearing Versace and linen, waving Rolex watches in the sky, or "money hanging out the anus."

At Tramps, as derogatory hoots and hollers from the De La Soul audience continue for Lil' Kim (whose Junior M.A.F.I.A. collective hit big with "Get Money") and Foxy Brown (whose songs sing the sartorial praises of Coco Chanel and many other clothing designers), the shifting spirit of the times reveals itself: MC incumbents who run on the platform of materialism are about to be impeached, and the grassroots candidates for these offices are steering clear of fashion designers and big-money, big Willie relationships.

In order to keep things really real, though, materialism would have to be recognized for being as much of a hiphop culture staple as bragging and boasting, or (yes, RZA) sampling. At least as old as Run-D.M.C.'s gold-plated, hollowed-out dookie rope chains, or Kurtis Blow decked out in a tuxedo with Jheri curls beneath his top hat, money—in vast amounts—has always made the hiphop world go round.

"Ghetto fabulous—it's like having an edge with a lot of style and a lot of creativity. And you always have drama with it. 'Cause you're young, you're urban, you never did it before, so you don't know quite how to handle it. So there's drama that's gonna have to come with it. This is a very dramatic generation."

—Andre Harrell

YOU WANT DRAMA? How about those Lee jeans patches from back in the day? Unfounded rumors circulated throughout

Bronx public high schools in the fall semester of 1984 about free sneakers given away at stores in exchange for x-amount of Lee patches. So, to the mangled-lyric chant of a Tears for Fears tune ("Shout! Shout!/Lees are played out!"), bands of B-boys went ripping through hallways, tearing the backsides out of unsuspecting victims like duly deputized fashion police. There was retribution for not staying current with hiphop style back in the day.

Suffering from fifteen-year-old puppy love, one day I traveled from the Bronx to the tree-lined suburban streets of Elmont, Long Island, and experienced several boldfaced revelations, including this: Kids from around my way took pains to appear moneyed, and kids from the 'burbs wanted badly to look broke. White, toothbrush-scrubbed, shell-toed Adidas gave way after two-hour bus and train rides to beat-up, scrawled-on Converses in dingy shades of gray. Iron-pressed pairs of fifty-dollar two-toned AJ jeans worn at the handball courts of the Bronx were a peculiarity to Green Acres mall-rats in faded twenty-dollar Levi's with holes worn through the knees.

Is it remotely possible that these highly style-conscious teens, maturing into the black twenty-somethings of the hiphop generation, retained their high-fashion fixations? Hiphop culture in the eighties had its own materialistic trappings; MCs like Jay-Z ("Being broke is childish/And I'm quite grown") were quite enamored of articles of old-school adornment such as sheepskin jackets, leather bubble goose-down coats, Cazal sunglasses, Nissan Maximas, Kangol hats, one-hundred-dollar-plus Air Jordan sneakers, Bally's shoes. In 2004, preoccupation with cellular phones, Hummers, and BlackBerry two-way pagers is not the spawn of Bad Boy Entertainment or Roc-a-Fella Records; it may just be a natural progression for a full-grown culture of folk with bigger bank accounts.

"Our initial direction as Public Enemy was to market nationalism. Our concept was to wear African leather medallions or something other than gold because people were getting their heads taken off for gold back then. We knew that if our people were going to be trendy, we could at least make it trendy to have them learn about themselves and their history . . . . People call hiphop a culture. Hiphop is a subculture. Black people's culture is culture. Our whole existence is culture."

—Chuck D

MY GREAT-GRANDPA JOHNSON was a longtime deacon at Harlem's Gospel Temple Church of America. Shaking off early-morning lethargy and lamenting the passing of Sunday-morning cartoons, I attended an occasional service with my parents back in my single-digit youth. Under my drowsy circumspection were the wooden pews, colorful stained-glass windows, and hand-held fans adorned with the images of virtuous church girls or the Reverend Martin Luther King Jr. More relevant, I noticed the dress of the worshipers: broad-brimmed, often elaborately styled hats and elegantly puritanical dresses on the women; handsome yet unyielding suits on the men. Sunday best. Easters were especially voguish—my young cousins and I always wore brand-new suits, which we were certain to outgrow by the following Easter. Church was the social life for many migrated Southern blacks who worked diligently six days a week, accounting in part for the grand visual display. Black materialism spans back to civil-rights-era baby boomers and back further to zoot-suited Harlemites of the jazz age. America is the birthplace of custom-tailored gangsters and *Dynasty* and *Dallas*, and of the snooty material elitism displayed in Tom Wolfe's *The Bonfire of the Vanities*. And since the beginning, mainstream black America has inevitably acceded to wealth's influence. If hiphop culture is negatively beset by materialism, it's essential to dig a little deeper before placing the blame on P. Diddy, Jay-Z, or Baby, the Cash Money Records' MC responsible for "bling-bling."

In his essay "Greed Is Only the Beginning," Black Arts movement writer Haki R. Madhubuti wonders, "Where are the serious rich among our people who are concerned about the vast majority of black people? It is sad to say there are tens of thousands of black people in the United States with serious money, skills, and talent who do nothing except compete in the Western race for conspicuous-consumption champions. The money that black people earn in the U.S. stays in the black community for about four hours. The real dilemma among most blacks with money is that of values."

This is why sociopolitical purists of the hiphop nation boo Sean Combs.

Don't knock me for trying to bury
Seven zeros over in Rio Dijanery
Ain't nobody's hero . . .
—P. Diddy, "It's All About the Benjamins"

GO MAKE OF ALL DISCIPLES

C AN WE FIND FLASH?"
    The International Hiphop Conference for Peace convenes at six o'clock on Wednesday, May 16, 2001, in the Secretariat Building of the United Nations, in Manhattan. Meridian Entertainment distributed nine hundred invitations—verbal, formal, and electronic—to MCs, DJs, breakers, graf artists, hiphop pioneers, rap media, photographers, hiphop historians, mainstream media, and international delegates. Roughly three hundred responded to the call. The Delegates Dining Room, Room 414, accommodates only two hundred seventy-five. Behind a table at the hall's entrance college-age female volunteers wearing black Temple of Hiphop T-shirts circulate leaflets of information to attendees as they arrive. Messages are included from the United Nations Educational, Scientific and Cultural Organization (UNESCO) Director-General Koïchiro Matsuura and United Nations Secretary-General Kofi Annan concerning peace and nonviolence, along with a U.N. General Assembly resolution proclaiming 2001–2010 the International Decade for a Culture of Peace and Nonviolence for the Children of the World, and a schedule of events for the Temple of Hiphop's fourth annual Hiphop Appreciation Week.

Bathed in the slight sunlight glowing through large windows, the assembled converse in clusters throughout the area. Some nurse small trays of fresh vegetable hors d'oeuvres and glasses of Chardonnay. The crowd includes celebrated hiphop photographer Ernie Paniccioli with his twenty-one-year-old daughter, Melissa; Rock Steady Crew Senior Vice President Jorge Pabón a/k/a Popmaster Fabel and his wife, Christie Z-Pabón; Harry Allen, writer and recognized "media assassin"; MCs Kurtis Blow, Roxanne Shanté, and Chuck D; hiphop archivist Ralph McDaniels; Meridian Entertainment founders Harry D'Janite and Lisa Patterson; pioneers Kool DJ Herc and Grandmaster Flash; and the prime organizer of the conference, KRS-One.

"Still no Flash. Is Flash here yet?"

As salmon is served at seven o'clock brief opening remarks are delivered by Harry Allen, then the Deputy Director of UNESCO's New York office, Alfatih Hamad. (The request of moderator/co-organizer Thembisa Mshaka for Grandmaster Flash goes unanswered. The DJ has left the United Nations.) Gravely serious at the lectern moments later, Ernie Paniccioli speaks to the assembly of dignitaries and hiphop figures. "The house is out of order," he says. "We who dwell on this planet have disrespected, destroyed, and undervalued every culture we have ever encountered. Hiphop culture is just the latest casualty. We do, I believe, have time left to save, salvage, preserve, restore, and correct it. That is and must be the main goal of the Temple of Hiphop, to identify and document what this culture is, where it came from, who its pioneers, visionaries, heroes were and are." He cites the formation of the Temple of Hiphop and the drafting of the Hiphop Declaration of Peace as vital steps for the survival of hiphop culture and declares, "In order to survive, a culture must have history, rules, laws, traditions, rituals, goals, and leaders. All of these things must come from within the family, not outside that family."

Part Native American of Cree heritage, Ernie Paniccioli concludes with a plea to respect Mother Earth. His closing environmental message concerns the melting polar ice caps and global warming. "I suggest to you tonight that all of that instant information and our instant communication and our cell phones and our two-ways and all this stuff will mean nothing unless we visit the tops of these mountains and see that the snow levels on the mountains of the earth are shrinking. Without snow, no rain. Without rain, no water. Without water, no life. In order for hiphop to survive you must have life. Peace and power." He leaves the podium to raucous applause.

Months ago Lawrence Parker a/k/a KRS-One deliberated with his wife, Pastor Simone G. Parker, and the publicists of Hiphop Appreciation Week, Meridian Entertainment's Harry D'Janite and Lisa Patterson, over how best to decriminalize hiphop culture in the court of public opinion. One of the most socially conscious MCs from the late-1980s political period of rap music, KRS-One was troubled over the recent murders (2Pac, the Notorious B.I.G., Big L) and incarcerations (Ol' Dirty Bastard, 50 Cent, Ghostface) in hiphop. Though every cultural movement contains rebellious, antiauthoritarian elements, KRS-One believes that "in other cultures the world is able to get information about those cultures' philosophers, inventors, discoverers, authors, and business people. If hiphop is to expand and grow, we— the philosophers, inventors, discoverers, authors, and business people—must begin the necessary process of decriminalizing rap music's public image, whereby hiphop can be given the proper documentation in world history." A proposal was drafted for Judy Duncan—head of the Ribbon International, a non-governmental organization affiliated with the United Nations—outlining a ceremony to take place at the U.N. proclaiming hiphop an international culture for peace. A meeting followed with the U.N. Secretary-General Kofi Annan's Deputy Press Secretary Chikahito Hasada, Judy Duncan, KRS-One, Harry D'Janite, Lisa Patterson, and members of UNESCO, an organization committed to promoting peace and nonviolence for worldwide youth.

"UNESCO and Kofi Annan's press secretary were blown away," KRS-One tells me several years later in January 2004. "And so they said, 'Let's do this, this is real.' What turned them on was that they recognized that hiphop as a cultural movement is in every country in the world. And it was advantageous to the United Nations to host an event like this because it gave them street credibility. Believe it or not, this is what we are discussing at the table at UNESCO: street credibility!" Raising the necessary sixty-five thousand dollars to hold an event at the Delegates Dining Room of the U.N. (a sum split between the owners of Lugz Footwear and KRS-One), a ceremony was conceived for a Hiphop Declaration of Peace document to be ratified during the fourth annual Hiphop Appreciation Week sponsored by KRS-One's Temple of Hiphop organization.

Kool DJ Herc is present. Grandmaster Flash is briefly present before abruptly taking flight. Afrika Bambaataa is absent. Speaking on behalf of the Universal Zulu Nation, Jorge Pabón a/k/a Popmaster Fabel is introduced following Ernie Paniccioli. "In this quest for peace, the Universal Zulu Nation continues to promote knowledge, wisdom, overstanding, freedom, justice, equality, peace, love, unity, respect, work, fun, overcoming the negative to the positive, and other core principles," Popmaster Fabel begins. "These rules have become the reality within the Universal Zulu Nation and it's clearly demonstrated by our international attendings and representatives at our yearly anniversaries.

Our chapters are scattered throughout the world, yet bound together through an overstanding and respect of each other's individual cultures as well as our common culture known as hiphop. The Universal Zulu Nation is also united, as we are today, in spirit and purpose. Our concerns for upliftment of all people are shared by many, as in evidence at this gathering and other conferences designed to highlight the positive power and potential of hiphop culture."

Popmaster Fabel speaks of the culture's Caribbean, African-American, and Latino roots, and its ability to attract followers of all faiths and nationalities. He is applauded when he remarks that "for the true hiphoppas, our standards have never changed regarding who is down by law and who isn't," and encouraged to repeat the phrase. Sticking to his message, he connects peacekeeping to a respect for differing opinions and viewpoints, with the audience at rapt attention. Hiphop culture, says Popmaster Fabel, has provided an opportunity for hiphoppas to explore the world and change many lives.

"The outcome of these efforts often brings about the strong conscious generation of individuals who have found peaceful ways to settle differences and who stand for the upliftment of their community. Unfortunately, hiphop culture has been misrepresented by the media and those who are either ignorant or have a hidden agenda. In this quest for peace we shouldn't depend solely on the media for its information about hiphop culture." No journalists or editors from any hiphop magazines are present at the International Hiphop Conference for Peace; the only writers present are Harry Allen and myself. "We should not rely on sources who have no authority, knowledge, or overstanding regarding hiphop's culture, origin, and evolution." Applause surges through the room. "We should make it our business to research, cross-reference, and fact-check all of the pieces to this great puzzle. With this we can become students of the culture. Ultimately I have found that the most honorable teachers continue to be great students. Peace!" Cries of "Zulu!" follow Popmaster Fabel to his table.

The moderator calls Ernie Paniccioli back to the podium; his stirring introduction and an audience ovation bring on the master of ceremonies, KRS-One. No speech seems imminent. KRS-One sincerely thanks all for attending and wants to move straight into a reading of the Hiphop Declaration of Peace as the ceremony remains on schedule. Diane and Larry Miller, the presidents of Lugz Footwear, are encouraged to stand, applauded for their forty-thousand-dollar donation to the conference. KRS-One rebukes MTV for refusing economic support when approached. "This public safety issue is very simple," says the MC. "It is that if all day long on radio and television and print media, if all you see is people like myself and yourself depicted as criminals in these magazines with no other reference, when our innocent brothers and sisters walk down the street and they dress the way we dress in the video or they talk the way we talk, they are immediately labeled criminal. And we talk constantly about racial profiling, rapper profiling, just the injustice of law enforcement in general, and a lot of these fingers are being pointed outward, outward. *Them, that, they.* This is about us right here. This is about us."

Susan Clark of UNESCO is asked to stand, to applause; then the Ribbon International's Judy Duncan. Next, KRS-One directs attention to the Hiphop Declaration of Peace.

A rather huge document drafted on oaktag by the Tats Cru, the Hiphop Declaration of Peace, KRS-One explains, consists of twenty-nine principles contributed by a consortium of different hiphop thinkers including Harry Allen, Ernie Paniccioli, and Russell Simmons. The document sits in the center of the Delegates Dining Room, fully sketched out but not entirely completed. "That's the point to the document itself: it's not finished," he says. "This is a rough draft to some of the collective views toward peace that we already share in our community. We will argue about this document for a year. Argue the validity of it, get some civil-rights heads in on it, get some criminal-law heads in on it, get some entertainment views as well as other people's opinions on this for a year. In 2002 the document closes and will open again in 2004 for additions." (By 2003 the Hiphop Declaration of Peace is narrowed down to a core eighteen principles.) KRS-One then proceeds to read the first ten principles of the declaration. (The version marked official is posted at Templeofhiphop.org.)

The signing commences. "I'm going to call up now the first name that should be on that document: our father, Kool DJ Herc." Manic applause rings out. "This man is the father of what we do. We respect you dearly, Herc. All photographers, please take note. Right along with Kool Herc, I'd like to call up my friend and colleague Chuck D of Public Enemy. Grandmixer D.XT, will you step to the document please? Pee Wee Dance, can you step to the document please? The Cold Crush Brothers, can you step to the document please? Grandmaster Caz, Eazy AD, KayGee, Tony Tone. Kurtis Blow, can you please step to the document? Doug E. Fresh, where are you? Please step to the document."

A line forms before the Hiphop Declaration of Peace, regulated somewhat by a Temple of Hiphop volunteer. As I sign the document, activist James Mtume delivers the final speech of the evening; the din of the crowd grows louder. A fifty-four-year-old veteran of the music industry, Mtume casts the most critical eye on the proceedings of all the speechmakers. "There's one thing I'd like to cover that hasn't been covered," he begins. "When we talk about culture, there seems to be an absence of the words 'politics' and 'power.' Culture's not just music, it's not just art, it's not just history, it's not just mythology. And one of the things that has been very absent with all the movements that we've been dealing with is the absence of a political movement, in particular among the hiphop youth." Antsy from successive speeches and the spectacle of the signing, the hiphop community and international delegates alike have become noisier; James Mtume asks for their silence, then continues. "I've been doing this for a long time. And one of the biggest games that has been run is conversations about music without conversations about control. You got to make a distinction between influence and power." The few paying attention applaud. "Influence is the ability to affect a thing. Power is the ability to change it. Right now we ain't changing nothing." The applause grows louder this time. "And in this document is the first step to something legitimate and something real. One thing that we got to have here the next time we come together is young hiphop artists who really need to understand what the peace document is about."

The room is back at attention and applauding full force. No record-charting, commercially relevant, popular MCs are present at the United Nations ceremony. "The next step is we got to get those who are fighting. Imamu Baraka said something very brilliant in his book, *Blues People*. He said, 'If you wanna know where the black people are at any time in this sojourn in America, listen to the music of that period.' Right now there's a division, not just between older blacks and younger blacks. You got a division now between the construct of hiphop. If we want to stop the booty-shaking on the videos . . . See, commenting on something is one thing, changing it is another. One of the things that we haven't dealt with is how we've allowed ourselves to be degradated [*sic*]. See, you can't always blame the outside forces here. They ain't making them videos if we ain't rejecting them. I wanna end real short because I know there's a signing going on. I wanna leave you with this one African proverb [for] people who don't want to contribute or don't want to participate in something. It says, 'He or she who sits in the middle of the room is hit by traffic going both ways.' " With that, Mtume leaves the podium to more applause. The International Hiphop Conference for Peace concludes at eight-thirty.

MERIDIAN ENTERTAINMENT CIRCULATED the Hiphop Declaration of Peace as a 17" x 11" document to the hiphop media during 2003; copies were likewise passed out at the thirtieth anniversary of the Universal Zulu Nation that November. Twenty-six faces adorn the certificate: figures like Afrika Bambaataa, Kool Moe Dee, and Kool DJ Herc. Grandmaster Flash is not pictured on the document. In January 2004 KRS-One explains why.

"He walked out of the U.N.," he says. "He felt hiphop should not be unionized. He felt that hiphop should not be institutionalized. He said, quote, 'I don't care what happens to hiphop. It should be free for whatever. Whatever happens to it just happens.' I said, 'Well, that's your opinion.' I invited him to the United Nations. He came. He was there. And then he said to me, 'I can't speak.' And I said, 'Why?' He said, 'I just . . . I don't agree. I don't agree with any of this.' And I said, 'Flash, we've been to summit after summit after summit, and we done beefed, we done argued, we done said what the white man done stole. All this stuff. Now we at the U.N. And here's our opportunity to document in world history what hiphop is and what its purpose and meaning is, and who you are in it. And you don't wanna get up there and say you're the inventor of scratching, cutting, and the mixer?' He said, 'No.' I said, 'Flash, they're ripping our children off with *your* invention.' He said, 'I don't care; that's not my concern.' And after we had our conversation, he said, 'Okay, okay, I'ma do it.' He got up and walked out. And so I said, out of respect to him, he won't be on the document."

KRS-ONE, BORN LAWRENCE BROWN in Brooklyn in 1965 (rechristened Lawrence Parker when his mother remarried, and later nicknamed Kris), is a burly figure—milk-chocolate complected with shoulder-length dredlocks and a broad nose, he's a man of great mirth (smiling widely in animated conversation) and great menace (scowling onstage fearsomely). From the very beginning of his rap career he has proclaimed himself "the teacher" of the hiphop community. Well-read and self-taught, KRS-One has long considered himself a philosopher and metaphysician. (His MC name, originally a graffiti tag, is an acronym for "knowledge reigns supreme over nearly everyone.") Raised in Brooklyn till the age of sixteen, he fled his mother's household and slept homeless in public parks pursuing a career as an MC.

Fate led the teenager to the Franklin Armory Men's Shelter in the Bronx and a social worker named Scott Sterling. One of the earliest rap casualties, Scott Sterling a/k/a DJ Scott La Rock partnered with KRS-One to form Boogie Down Productions (for Boogie Down Bronx) in 1986, launching a livelihood off of the inner-city anthem "South Bronx." (Scott La Rock was shot dead in 1987 at twenty-five, attempting to mediate a dispute between Boogie Down Productions affiliate D-Nice and an ex-girlfriend's boyfriend outside of a South Bronx housing project.) A socially conscious, proudly intelligent MC, KRS-One delivered college-tour lectures at Harvard, Yale, and elsewhere in the late 1980s and early 1990s, while releasing albums and spearheading movements such as Stop the Violence and H.E.A.L. (Human Education Against Lies). His ruminations on how to organize hiphop culminated in 1996 with the creation of the Temple of Hiphop, a preservation society designed for the upliftment and promotion of the culture.

"For me, it started in 1987 with a meeting that Afrika Bambaataa had," says KRS-One, tracing the origin of the Temple of Hiphop, "a roundtable discussion he had in Latin Quarters [nightclub]. And in that meeting he called for hiphop's unity. Everybody was there: Daddy-O, Heavy D, MC Lyte, Biz Markie, everybody of that '87 era. And so I went and started this concept of creating an organized body for hiphop, just an organized group of people who are going to make a commitment to make sure that hiphop is presented to the world correctly. Not that we have a judgment on it. Not that we're gonna say, 'This is correct hiphop.' We don't wanna take that stance, like, 'This is real hiphop and that's fake hiphop.' But we do wanna take the stance of, 'We *are* hiphop and we are not a product.' In other words, to sell your product, you're gonna have to have some respect for us as a people and that organized body. Sort of the Humane Society for hiphop."

Jive Records' Vice President of Artist Development Ann Carli and writer Nelson George arranged an all-star hiphop anti-violence benefit song titled "Self Destruction" in 1988, after concertgoer Julio Fuentes was stabbed to death for his gold chain at a rap show at Long Island's Nassau Coliseum. As a recording artist for Jive Records with his own song called "Stop the Violence," KRS-One was approached to guide the Stop the Violence Movement. The profits from "Self Destruction," some four hundred thousand dollars, were donated to the National Urban League. "I spearheaded this movement Stop the Violence—at least for a minute I thought I did, until I started making demands and quickly realized that I was an artist on the project. That's how the money got sent to the National Urban League. I had voted for a school at that time."

The next stage in creating a movement of his own involved Elektra Records and a project called Human Education Against Lies (H.E.A.L.). An album under the banner of the H.E.A.L. organization was meant to generate revenue for the publication of a book called *The Gospel of Hiphop*, sixteen million free copies of which were to be distributed to urban youth. "So right around this whole thing, I'm figuring out how to lead a culture," he recalls. "And I'm saying to myself, I see leadership all around me but no one's leading. Everyone's pointing at me. Herc: 'Yo Kris, I'll back you.' Afrika Bambaataa. 'Yo Bam, what's up with Zulu Nation?' 'Yo Kris, we'll back you.' It got to the point where I'm like, it seems like I'm the only one that's gonna organize. Around this time of H.E.A.L., I realized that I am going to have to step into a leadership role because I'm humbly looking at others first and saying, 'Why don't you lead? What's up with you?' But no one could see the vision then of hiphop as an organized body of people, as a community. We put this whole thing together so that we could complete what is now called *The Gospel of Hiphop* and put it out, but that didn't happen. Elektra dropped the ball on the project and it was very political. Everybody, they turned their back. 'What is he trying to do? Unionize hiphop?' "

The word *culture* has the stem of *cult* within it. KRS-One's activities may have messianic overtones, groping to establish a long-lasting hiphop civilization out of hiphop culture, but he seems well aware of the potential opposition to his intentions. Nonbelievers accuse KRS-One of trying to turn hiphop into a church, to systematize a culture born out of railing against the system to begin with. His orthodoxy seems extremist to those most comfortable with hiphop as a spontaneous, rebellious body of expression. Cultures start preservation movements when people see something valuable disappearing. Grandmaster Flash walked out of the

United Nations in the midst of a celebration for the culture he himself spawned over such objections. Yet KRS-One realizes his ideals will not appeal to everyone. *The Gospel of Hiphop*—a study manual for bourgeoning cultural specialists containing hiphop's philosophies and authoritative history—will be dispensed exclusively to Temple of Hiphop members in 2005, intended as an accumulation of the hiphop wisdom of the past thirty years. Paragraphs are numbered, not unlike the Holy Bible. R-31 of a section of *The Gospel of Hiphop* subtitled "The First Overstanding: The Refinitions" defines the rap fan:

> A Rap fan is anyone who enjoys or respects Rap music. Rap fans are only interested in watching or listening to Rap music even though they may call it Hip Hop. To the Rap fan Hiphop is music. Rap fans are culturally and spiritually blind, deaf, and dumb to Hiphop . . . The deeper spiritual lessons and Overstandings of the Temple of Hiphop are incomprehensible to them and can cause the Rap fan unnecessary suffering. Be careful when teaching Rap fans. It is best to keep it simple.

The Temple of Hiphop is not for rap fans. Yet and still, Grandmaster Flash is no rap fan and he abandoned the effort to institutionalize hiphop based on ideological differences. And when hiphop begins to feel like school or church, even hiphop fans may blanch. "I absolutely agree," KRS-One diplomatically responds. "Here's how we get around the problem. First of all, the right person has to institutionalize the culture. It's a general statement, that, 'If you institutionalize the culture, you take away its vibrancy, its spontaneity, its rebelliousness, you kill it, it's like trying to catch a butterfly.' But that's a general thing. Who are we talking about who's going to institutionalize the culture, if it's not us? Can't nobody from the outside institutionalize it. They can't do it. No one will respect that. There are only a few people who *can* do it, who are intimate enough to know that, to agree and say, 'We *cannot* institutionalize hiphop and kill its spontaneity; we cannot do that.'

"I believe the spontaneous hiphop is balanced by organized hiphop. Spontaneous hiphop is not the all to hiphop, and neither is ordered hiphop. The argument within the question is that those of us that want to organize hiphop are gonna take away its spontaneity. We have freestyled the culture for thirty years! Eventually the freestyle ends, as every MC knows. Eventually you start sounding stupid. We cannot freestyle the culture any longer, not while hiphoppas are thirty and forty with children. Not while hiphoppas are dying. Jam Master Jay is because we're freestyling the culture. Had there been some order to the culture—meaning health insurance—where Jam Master Jay maybe would not have to hustle on the side . . . Where's the organized body that comes to Jay and says, 'Listen, we'll buy your house, we have a kitty of a million dollars for issues just like this'? Now to do that, we have to organize the culture. Organization does not mean the death of spontaneity or creativity or the rebellious nature."

All this philosophizing went into the establishment of the Temple of Hiphop. Operating as a secret society since 1994 ("It was just me and Harry [Allen], Chuck D, Fat Joe, Kid Capri, Rampage, and a couple of cats talking about it"), KRS-One announced the organization on the New York City Hot 97 *Street Soldiers* call-in show of radio personality Lisa Evers in 1996. With *I Got Next*, the career crest of KRS-One's mainstream popularity in 1997, a Temple of Hiphop registration form was included in the packaging, constituting a cultural survey. Eighty thousand registration forms provided answers to "How were you introduced to hiphop?" and "How can the Temple of Hiphop help you?"

"Hiphop is the name of our collective consciousness, and we get that first definition from our membership," he says. "People mailed in and the most widely used description of hiphop amongst people that don't even know each other is that it is a conscious movement, a movement of consciousness. Beyond race, beyond religion, beyond occupation, beyond class, it's a movement of consciousness; hiphop brings people together. That's what the whole world said. And so we took that as a banner."

KRS-One instituted the first annual Hiphop Appreciation Week in 1998, inspired by author Carter G. Woodson's Negro History Week (later the Black History Month of February), to foster a common spirit among hiphop adherents. In honor of the May 19 birthday of Malcolm X, the third week of May is designated for the celebration, meditation, and contemplation of hiphop heritage. In New York City, a ceremony was held in the Main Chamber of City Hall on May 14, 2001, where Bronx Borough President Fernando Ferrer issued a proclamation to that effect:

> Whereas: Hiphop culture, which originated in the Bronx, is a lifestyle for countless people around the world which unites and establishes a common identity; it was developed with the purpose of ensuring health, love, awareness, and wealth for ourselves, our children and our children's children forever . . . Now, therefore, I, Fernando Ferrer, do hereby proclaim every third week in May herein Hiphop Appreciation Week.

For the past several years KRS-One has been crisscrossing the country establishing meeting houses—temples—for discussion groups and courses on what he and the Temple of Hiphop consider hiphop's *nine* elements: breaking, emceeing, deejaying, graf art, street knowledge, beatboxing, street fashion, street language, and street entrepreneurialism. Quietly, KRS-One has been nation building.

THE TOWN HALL MEETING (topic: "Hiphop—Its Meaning and Purpose") for the fourth annual Hiphop Appreciation Week begins at nine o'clock P.M. on Saturday, May 19, 2001, at Riverside Church in Harlem. Nearly two hundred people sway back and forth in the pews, arms raised above heads, chanting in call-and-response unison under the direction of spiritualist Dr. Camille Yarborough. "We're born of the old sea. We're born of the deep root. We're born of the tall grass. We are the sweet fruit of the African sea . . ." This goes on for about five minutes and ends with everyone turning to the person next to him or her with an "I love you."

Those assembled include Harry Allen, record producer Prince Paul, and poet Liza Jessie Peterson. On the elevated stage stand Wise Intelligent, Grandmixer D.XT, Chuck D, and KRS-One. The crowd shouts out "Ache!" after each name spoken by Yarborough as she pours out libations for the deceased members of the hiphop community. DJ Scott La Rock, Cowboy, Grandmaster Flowers, the Notorious B.I.G., Trouble T-Roy, the Human Beatbox, MC Trouble, Pumpkin, Keith Haring, Prince Messiah, Disco King Mario, Lesley Pitts, Eazy-E, DJ Junebug, TCD, Mercury, Sugar Shaft, Scientifik, Stretch, Charizma, Cliff 159, Masterdon, Dondi White, Seagram, Big L, Big Punisher, Freaky Tah, and Tupac Shakur are among those honored in this ceremony, water poured off into a plant's soil after the calling of each name as an African drummer plays a hushed rhythm.

Hostess April Silver thanks Camille Yarborough for her contribution to the evening, and calls Grandmixer D.XT to the microphone, enumerating his accomplishments as a hiphop pioneer (including winning a Grammy Award for scratching on Herbie Hancock's 1983 "Rockit"). Stepping to the podium, Grandmixer D.XT immediately begins speaking to the topic of racism and white supremacy, apropos for the seventy-sixth birthday of Malcolm X. "We cannot deal with the culture of hiphop unless we deal with white supremacy, because all of the issues we have in hiphop are a direct result of white supremacy. The hiphop culture indirectly comes from suppression and oppression and depression. Y'all hear me?" The audience responds. The United States is a violent society, says D.XT, denouncing the mainstream media's condemnation of hiphop violence while they turn a blind eye to the genocide of Native Americans and other atrocities in American history. He detours into an evaluation of racial profiling before segueing into the topic of the evening: the meaning and purpose of hiphop.

"Here we are, faced with the question of what hiphop is and what do we do with hiphop. And yes, I'm one of the cats who was there with that energy that came before as rock 'n' roll, and came before as jazz, came before as blues, came before as classical music, for those that don't know that the Moors brought that to Europe." Applause. "And so yes, I am one of the revolutionaries of hiphop. And for me to stand here today and talk to you about this, I realize that I can't lie. Hiphop is truly about keeping it real. So we have a responsibility, that's where hiphop is now. Hiphop's responsibility is to do everything that it possibly can to eradicate this concept of white supremacy." Applause. "Keeping it real, we need to deal with some of these issues. We're at a very critical point on this planet. If we look at the planet and we use our African eyes to see the world, we will clearly see that we are in a very serious situation. Something is killing the planet. Something is killing the ozone. Something is killing the sea. Something is killing human beings. Something is killing mankind. What we need to do now is use hiphop to eradicate these ideas of white supremacy." Applause. "I thank you, and I would like to end in challenging everyone in this room, because there is nobody in this room whose genetic makeup did not originate on the continent of Africa." ("Speak on it!" a woman's voice yells out.) "So it is our responsibility in hiphop—whether you're white, black, whatever—keep it real: White supremacy is played out."

Wise Intelligent speaks next. As the most charismatic MC of the Poor Righteous Teachers, a popular black nationalist group from hiphop's golden age, it is expected that Wise Intelligent will pick up on Grandmixer D.XT's theme. "In my opinion," he begins, "there's multiple purposes to hiphop. A lot of people will say it's a form of expression. Hiphop definitely gives a voice to those whose spirit has been broken through poverty or oppression. A while ago, we couldn't say what we had to say. Nobody even really knew we exist or what was going on in the neighborhoods that we live in. I come from projects in Trenton, New Jersey. I remember having two pairs of pants, shared 'em with my brothers. When Kris made that song 'Love's Gonna Get Cha,' talking about how he was sharing the outfit with cousins, that's my life. That's where I came from." Wise Intelligent, the youngest of all the speakers scheduled, is a father. He laments that hiphop is used to push negative images on the youth, and cleverly links the promotion of nihilistic behavior through entertaining rap music to the growing prison population in the United States.

"The number one business in America, in my opinion, is the prison industry. They're tearing down the parks with the basketball courts, they're building prisons and courthouses. Rappers don't understand that the climate is being set to fill the jail, the prisons. And we are the most likely candidates to fill those prisons." Applause. "To take it a little bit further, right now in hiphop, bling-bling is the new big-money thing. Everybody's rocking ice, everybody has diamonds.

But we never think about that diamond that's grown in Sierra Leone." Applause. "That kid whose arms are being amputated by warlords who are doing whatever it takes to get those diamonds and send them into the international diamond trade where they end up in all these diamond jewelers down here in New York. And we go and buy it. We go and buy a one-hundred-twenty-seven-thousand-dollar piece that we could be feeding a lot of babies with." Applause.

"As far as a solution to our problems go, I don't know what the solution is. But I know it has a lot to do with the lack of knowledge of knowing who we really are." Applause. "I know that for a fact 'cause I look at other nations. I look at the Koreans. They come over here from Korea with a goal: to further and better their peoples. When they come over here and set up a store in our community, they sell *us* chicken wings. We don't have stores in their communities. They don't live in our community. They come here, they set up shop, they get money to send their kids to N.Y.U. off of selling us chicken wings. Then they bring more Koreans from Korea and they do the same thing and they repeat the cycle. They build up their people and they build up their nation." Far from prejudicially condemning Koreans, Wise Intelligent seemingly regrets that African Americans haven't yet implemented a similar plan. "The Jewish people, they do the same exact thing. The Jewish community is all Jewish. The schools are run by Jewish people. The hospitals are Jewish hospitals. The children are in Jewish education. But in our community, we don't own the stores, we don't run the schools, we don't run the police precinct, therefore we suffer. That's the beginning of our problems." (KRS-One remarks in our subsequent discussion: "I take hiphop serious in the sense that it can be a real culture, like Greek, like German or Jamaican. Actually, to be more accurate, like Jews in that sense. A sect of people around a principle.")

Wise Intelligent decries the miseducation taking place in the public school system before swaying back on message. "Hiphop does have a purpose. Hiphop is like manna was to the Israelites when they were in the wilderness. When they were hungry and they had nothing to eat, and they cried to God and God said, 'Okay, I'm gonna feed you,' and bread fell from the heavens. That's what hiphop's purpose is: it's feeding the poor people." (R-24:2 of *The Gospel of Hiphop* states: "Spiritually, Hiphop is God's response to us. It is how God saved our kind. It is the strategy God used and still uses to save our kind.") He iterates that he and the Poor Righteous Teachers always represented the have-nots through their music. Like James Mtume at the Declaration of Peace Signing Ceremony, he bemoans the absence of high-profile entertainers like Jay-Z and DMX at Riverside Church, but refuses to condemn them. "We can't take shots at them, we can't down them. They're our brothers. And every revolution, I've learned, needs finance. And those brothers right there . . ." The audience laughs, then steadfastly applauds. Wise Intelligent launches into an appeal for blacks to learn their own cultural history beyond hiphop before entering into a questionable tirade about the nature of whites. The spirit of Malcolm X moves on the audience.

"Us and white people are different." The crowd *mmmm*s. "I don't care what nobody say, I will argue that all the way to the Supreme Court." Laughter, applause. "We come from totally different makeups. We went through totally different processes to become who we are today. Not just slavery. You lose a lot of warm-heartedness caught up in the ice," he says, referring to the Caucasus Mountains, taught by some black nationalist groups to be the origin of European civilization. "We were like farmers, they're more like hunters. We're husbandmen, we raise minions and things of that nature. They came up out of caves and bust the first thing they saw on the head with a rock and ate it." Laughter erupts; another woman yells, "Speak on it!" "We really have to pay attention to that. A wild dog and a hyena don't mix. They're all dogs, though."

"A hyena's more cat-like!" someone shouts out.

"Whichever. Same difference," he responds.

(KRS-One distances himself from Wise Intelligent's separatist message afterwards in his own speech, mentioning: "Hiphop and black people need to die to themselves and be reborn. This concept of dying to yourself and being reborn as someone else, I believe, is one of the underlying solutions to the problem." In *Ruminations*, KRS-One's 2003 essay collection, he writes: "When it comes to solving the issue of racial equality in the United States, it seems that a member from every race, religion, and class is going to have to sacrifice themselves by dying to their race, religion, and class, to be reborn into a community of people that have also transcended their races, religions, and social statuses.")

Wise Intelligent continues unabated, jumping from rappers who represent ghetto lifestyles while living in the suburbs ("You gotta be able to distinguish what's real from what's fantasy"), to the civil-rights generation's abandonment of their hiphop progeny ("Right now, hiphop is a multimillion-dollar industry and our parents are nowhere around. When they come around, they're saying, 'Roll over rap music with a steamroller' "), to the importance of self-respect ("Teach the babies who they are, and then they'll respect themselves on their own"). He closes with a message of self-love. "I don't like the idea of even talking about white supremacy and a white man doing this and a white man doing that. It's up to us. The beginning of our problem [is] we don't know who we are." Applause. "Knowing who we are is our common denominator, whether your religion is Christianity, Islam, or whatever. When the Koreans come here, their common denominator is, they're Korean. The

Chinese, they're Chinese. That's why they're able to progress. We don't have anything to unite under, so how can we unite? How can we unite when Farrakhan is saying, 'Unite for me,' and then you got a Christian saying, 'I'm not a Muslim; I'm not down with that'? That's what our problem is, a lack of knowledge of self. We need to go to the library one day, all of us, and try to find out who we are, man, and dig up some of the lies they buried. Peace and love, y'all." Resounding applause booms from Riverside Church.

Chuck D imparts the closing remarks at nearly eleven o'clock. But before that ending comes, KRS-One delivers his final speech of the fourth annual Hiphop Appreciation Week, his third of the week following Monday's City Hall Proclamation Ceremony and Wednesday's United Nations Declaration of Peace Signing Ceremony. If KRS-One has his druthers, the audience facing him tonight will make up the budding citizenship of a new nation. The ultimate goal of the Temple of Hiphop, KRS-One's lifework, in fact, is the creation of a hiphop city, a hiphop Las Vegas not unlike early twentieth-century, all-black, preintegration towns like Eatonville, Florida. ("At that point I could just die," he says. "Then it's preserved. Our children and their children's children eat forever. And that's the point, really.") Those assembled tonight are potentially his tribe. He chooses his words carefully.

"This is the meaning of Hiphop Appreciation Week, to be able to come together as brothers and sisters and discuss the state of hiphop and where it comes from. Wise Intelligent just took it beyond a hiphop level, just started talking about black folk, which is extremely important in this discussion. I represent the philosophical aspect of hiphop culture. [Philosophers] always seem to talk about ideas that are really, I guess, in advance of what the public can understand. My job is to bring you what I call uncommon knowledge.

"You are seeing it happen. You have a choice. Out of all the sets of people you see in the world today, just think to yourself: What if I was at the beginning of their culture? What if I was at the beginning of their religion? What would I have said to Moses after he came out of the mountain and everybody was, 'Party!', and didn't care nothing about how they got to where they got? And here comes Moses with laws, and he's all caught up in God consciousness. He's just comin out the mountain and everybody's basically bling-blinging." The hiphop nation laughs.

"What would you say if you was there? This is where you are now right now. There is a movement happening before your very eyes, like that. You have to decide what side you're on, and what role you're gonna play. You can ignore it, you have that freedom. You could say, 'Look, I'm not a part of all of that hiphop. Just go 'head.' That's your choice. You can also say, 'Hey, look, I grew up with the culture. If I had my way, I'd say *this*.' The lives of your children is what's really at stake. Nothing we are doing here today is for us. We're try-ing to create a new nation to deal with some of the old prob-lems. You do have a choice. Your children have a choice. The choice here is: Am I going to be part of a new nation? Can I build onto a new nation? Am I conscious? Here's what it means, 'conscious.' Am I conscious of the reality of my pres-ence? Not my past, not my future. Where I am right now. Right now, we're in Riverside Church, one nation. Right now. You look at you here—all of you, here, are a new sect of people.

"Imagine this."

Scars of the Soul Are Why Kids Wear Bandages When They Don't Have Bruises

ARE THE REPORTS of hiphop's death greatly exaggerated?

1. POPMASTER FABEL: *"If we're talking about a culture then we should be talking about cultivating, we should be talking about growth, nurturing."*

Nostalgia can be a great persuader. Compelled by an inner impulse to romanticize the past, every generation unavoidably rhapsodizes about back in the day—an economic crisis and some world wars; fire hoses, police dogs, and marches for civil rights; plugging speakers into street lamps and bombing trains with graf. We all hold tightly to the familiar anecdotal narratives of our wonder years, those stories parents and grandparents routinely trot out at family gatherings, grating on nerves year after year. Hiphop is now long enough in the tooth that the eldest among us consider this modern age a pale deterioration of the seventies and eighties that birthed and shaped the culture.

Within the huge circle of those who casually buy rap music and watch rap videos, there is a smaller circle privy to the cultural arcana necessary to qualify them as citizens of the hiphop nation. (Stuff like always passing blunts on your left-hand side, or knowing how to convert headphones into a microphone, or holding dear memories of a youth spent either emceeing, deejaying, breaking, or bombing.) Inside this smaller circle is another subset, the hiphop purists, who can be found attending anniversary celebrations for the Universal Zulu Nation or the Rock Steady Crew—diehard adherents of the culture prone to debating its direction, pining for the good ol' days of DJ battles and music unbeholden to commercial dictates. Purists are a minority, made up largely of actual pioneers of the culture, non-American youth ascertaining the culture's value from a remove, and native New York City old-heads in our thirties and forties who recall firsthand what the culture was based on at the beginning.

For things to fall apart they must once have held together. The myth of hiphop's stable, coherent, idyllic past (myth, I say, because things were violent also) hinges partially on the community spirit of the park jams. Popmaster Fabel—popper/locker, Senior Vice President of the Rock Steady Crew, and dance instructor—addressed a sparse audience in Queens at the Jamaica Center for Arts and Learning during November 2003, a lecture entitled "The Great Hiphop Swindle" dealing with "how hiphop culture has been hijacked by the rap industry and how the culture was stripped apart little by little." Popmaster Fabel says, "Once the jams stopped, the cultural chain of succession was broken. The lack of jams deprives the community of their potential to network artistically and socially, and that really is when things started going really wrong. You had cultural gaps. The kids didn't know what to follow anymore; the kids weren't as inventive and artistic anymore. It was the age of video games and all that stuff started coming into the picture and we sort of lost the whole . . ."

He pauses.

"Well, we're continuously losing people who don't have

that kind of connection anymore to that cipher, to that intuitive essence of celebrating life, which is the jam."

Such are the personal and public consequences of the loss of history, that today the jams and block parties of the seventies exist no longer and their benefits are likewise lost to short communal memory. From Popmaster Fabel's purist p/o/v, hiphop "came from the cultural imperative, the fact that we needed to refresh ourselves no matter what." The culture was originally a community movement, our relationship to each other (black, Latino, poor peoples) and the motions we made for upliftment and expression. Yet hiphop was illegal. So whether or not positive effects resulted from mass public celebrations at Cedar Park, jacking electricity from lampposts and bum-rushing public spaces without permits was against the law. Authorities knocking this pillar of hiphop's foundation then considered park jams along the same lines as vandalizing graffiti. Folks affirming their presence in a world that insists they don't exist—with fat markers— could only be stigmatized as defacing public property. "What we're really talking about is the struggle for survival in the streets and a struggle for identity," Fabel says. "That's why we wore those [name-plate] belt buckles, that's why we wore our names all over the place. We were trying to let you know, 'This is who I am. This is my identity. This means something to me.' And it meant everything to us back then."

Central to Popmaster Fabel's lecture is the music business dicing up hiphop culture in the mid-eighties based on which elements turned a profit. "Once the rap industry started making all their money over the albums, little by little they started separating," he says. "The DJ was completely eliminated and replaced with a mini-disc or a DAT. Stylized art like graf, totally out of the picture. It was like, let's just take this thing here, the rapping and the guys who create the beats—which was the DJs at one point—and let's run with that 'cause we could make money off of that. What was once priceless now has a price. There's no measuring the benefits a culture can have on a community, if it's lived progressively. What we did and what I experienced as a kid growing up when hiphop was really hiphop is absolutely priceless. You just can't put money on it. And unfortunately, now it's sold really cheap."

Evolution requires ideas to unfold into higher states of manifestation. And every group of youngsters has its own way of responding to the environment they have inherited. I suggest that maybe today's youth has its own approach to dealing with the world that works better for them than the jams of old or practicing the traditional elements of hiphop. Fabel says he's just fine with that, as long as that approach is not called hiphop. The passing of an old order lives within his response. How many aspects of hiphop must change before it's no longer hiphop, before it evolves into something that requires a new name, with new founding principles to track? If hiphop is a community movement, then a rose by any other name still needs to satisfy its cultural imperative, to serve the needs of the community. I stand up for hiphop's heyday sometimes and hear the echo of my father getting hyped over old Motown choreography.

2. MUMs: "*Hopefully, hiphop has the ability to be much bigger than just something that can die from being oversaturated.*"

These are hiphop purist waters lapping at your feet. Most people don't consider the culture this deeply, and several who do take it this seriously—professors Michael Eric Dyson and Todd Boyd, for example—are too old to ever have executed a headspin. Let us wade in a little deeper with some questions. Did hiphop spring into being for the upliftment of poor peoples of color, for expressing ourselves. Is emceeing, in general, spoken affirmations, and are MC battles about whose affirmations can come off the most poetic. Is it infeasible for hiphop to be dead because the culture is a reflection of the people, and the people are not dead. Is hiphop still alive in those areas where it began in the first place, before its commercialization.

When taking the temperature of hiphop, it's important to know in which hole to stick the thermometer. From one p/o/v, hiphop is MCs rhyming, DJs spinning, B-boys breaking, bombers throwing up art; and the lack of public interest or participation in every single one of these elements proves a weakness of the overall culture. If these are your values, then social change has long since affected hiphop for the worse. Emceeing and deejaying are still relatively healthy, but spray-painting trains is now impossible and breaking isn't nearly as viable a modern pursuit for teens as PlayStation; from B-boys to Game Boys. From another p/o/v, hiphop is the entire approach to life of anyone born around and after 1965: Suge Knight's entrepreneurialism; Allen Iverson's braids, tattoos, and crossover dribble; Rakim's metaphysical philosophy; E-40's penchant for inventive slanguage; the Rocawear line's baggy jeans. Under this construction, urban culture itself equals hiphop culture, and not knowing that Bugaloo Sam invented the backslide (Michael Jackson's famous moonwalk) doesn't make you any less hiphop.

"Hiphop should be being hiphop, whatever that is," says Bronx native muMs—actor, poet, and playwright. "See, that's the quest. We don't know exactly what that is. What fuckin is it? 'Cause it's a lot bigger and broader than any of us actually thought it could be. So nobody knows exactly what it is. Until we figure out that, then I guess its first leader—if it chooses to have a leader, if it feels that it's that strong—will say then, 'This is what we should do.' But right now, it's in, like, bubbling stages." Purism splinters at this juncture of the argument. Because to be preservationist, one would say that hiphop already has a leader—Universal Zulu Nation founder Afrika Bambaataa—and that he's already issued instructions: "Take hiphop culture back into the peace, unity, love, and having fun." But to be speculative is to assume that we've barely scratched the surface of what the hiphop nation can become (what thirty-year-old nation has?) and that the urban population has yet to mobilize hiphop into a form that most effectively fulfills its purpose.

"I think the mainstreaming of hiphop is just this bump in the road of something bigger, hopefully," says muMs. In the confines of his Harlem apartment I ask if hiphop has lost its heart. "Has hiphop ever had a heart? What did hiphop ever really *really* care about, you know? If we go back to British Walker days, it's about the fame. It was about writing your name on the side of a train and hopefully that train would go to every borough, and everybody in every borough will know your name. And that's what it was about. I loved that."

Purists feel that the rap industry swooped in at this phase and began dividing hiphop's elements through capitalism. Speculative hiphop visionaries look at it differently. "Hiphop is a cultural envelope that's getting expanded by the growing money that's coming inside of its contents, so it's getting expanded in all these directions," muMs continues. "Yeah, we're seeing Tupac and Biggie die. That has got to be the worst of it. What can be the best of it? If hiphop is as strong as we hopefully believe that it is, yeah, it has a heart. It's still alive. Somebody needs to say, 'Let's structure this: Yea, now we structure this hiphop thing that we created in the Bronx.' *We* created," he adds, referring to our shared Bronx background.

Debating hiphop this way can lead to circuitous theorizing. Purists believe hiphop already has a structure (the four elements) and a leader (Afrika Bambaataa), and if you're essentially talking about mobilizing the urban populace, then you should call it something else besides hiphop. Speculationists, on the other hand, believe that just as hiphop came up from nothing to dominate the worldwide youth culture, it may continue to grow from here into a force capable of dominating other aesthetics of living (politics, spirituality)—and that in order to do this, a new structure and a new leader is necessary. Nelly records selling millions may be the least of it. What can be the most of it?

"What we need to do, we need to financially figure out a way to make money go back in our own community, and our community be part of this country that we own," says muMs. "We really need to see the structure of our country. That is what it's there for. It's there, we all went to school and learned that shit. So let us use it. You try to organize, you try to say, 'This is the Temple of Hiphop,' ain't nobody rushing to go join that. *So then, not calling it 'hiphop'* [italics mine]. Something needs to be organized, though. What they are joining, more and more every year, is Republicans and Democrats, right? If you make that shiny enough for half these motherfuckers out here that don't vote . . . 'Aiight, I'll vote for this nigga. I like this nigga, whatever. This nigga said he got designated places where you could smoke in the city on the ballot. I like that shit!' You ain't gonna do that! It ain't gonna happen, but word, just put it out there. Put out the idea. It's the trick but you get your people behind you. Then through that, your views will conflict with those of whatever people that you work with. You get large enough, a large contingent enough, you break off from Democrat and you become a leftist Democrat. Or a rightist Democrat. Or a leftist Republican. Then that's when we build."

3. ALEXANDRA PHANOR: "*I think young people who listen to rock 'n' roll are more appreciative of the Rolling Stones or the Doors and stuff; but in hiphop kids don't really care.*"

Not every black man, woman, and child of the civil-rights era belonged to the NAACP, SNCC, or SCLC organizations devoted to social change. Surely not every urban-sympathizing man, woman, and child of the hiphop nation will want to unite with the Hiphop Summit Action Network or the Universal Zulu Nation. Casual rap-music consumers clearly won't think it's that deep and even hiphop purists—preservationists as well as the more abstract speculationists—may have their objections to structuring the culture.

In 1997 Alexandra Phanor (along with partner Thea Habjanic) channeled her frustrations over the lack of exposure for underground hiphop into the creation of an independent 'zine, *One Love*. Since its passing she's concentrated on providing mainstream magazines with the type of cultural reporting *One Love* delivered, and lately has begun raising funds for a documentary on the Queensbridge housing projects (the breeding ground of Roxanne Shanté, DJ Marley Marl, Nas, Mobb Deep, and others). Phanor is a conscientious objector to formalizing hiphop. "I think things like that are going a little too far," she says. "And I see the point in preserving it because you want to make sure people remember the past. [But that's] doing exactly what the whole game was not supposed to be about. Like, becoming into this institution. It was just art." Referring to a thick information packet disseminated by the Temple of Hiphop (which included a membership certificate and definitions of hiphop's culture, history, and elements), Phanor says, "It's stupid. How dare you tell me what is? You can tell me about what's happened in the past, but don't tell me, like, if I don't follow these guidelines I'm not hiphop. What the hell are you? Trying to put everything in a box. How can you put it in a box?"

In her Brooklyn apartment blocks away from Marcy Houses, I ask if hiphop could benefit from organization of some sort.

"Yeah, definitely, I think it needs that right now."

Like, say, the Universal Zulu Nation?

"Well, it should be the Zulu Nation. But the thing about it is that I always think they don't have money to do much. They don't have money to do so much on a large scale, but they do stuff. I mean, I find out about different events they have, and people aren't really interested. They don't see it."

At a crowded Zulu Nation–sponsored panel discussion at the Bronx Museum of the Arts in November 2003, Chicago Zulu Nation chapter president Lord Cashus D remarked, "They be talking about how we need to all organize. No, we don't need to organize. We need to do some work, 'cause we already organized."

The true issue then becomes, what is the work of the hiphop nation? Popmaster Fabel says, "I think every person as an individual should take a minute to figure how they can pass the information on," information about the foundational principles of hiphop. MuMs says, "We have to kinda deal with what it is because if we let them dictate it, you see what it's turning into." So which is the work of hiphop, to preserve the history or to politick?

Of the preservationist tack, Alexandra Phanor says, "It's really sad; I think that there's no appreciation for the past in hiphop at all. When hiphop started it was such a new thing, they kept developing and developing and people were always on, 'What's the new thing?' And I think that's why people don't really care about the past, because there was always something new new new coming up. So people feel as though, who cares about what happened before? It moves so fast that it's like, 'That was ages ago. That's a whole different look, a different style, everything was like completely different.' When you watch TV, the only time they play old-school videos is during the old-school section. They should just play videos!" Of the political tack: "People are always out on their own agendas. Russell Simmons is one. I always get emails about all these things that he's doing. Everybody wants to put their flag down on what they organize, and it's not really about coming together and finding a solution. This is an industry where there's all these intelligent black men with money in their pocket. And you can't, all this time, come up with something, use your money towards doing something? The power that these people have? They just don't wanna do it. And the ones who wanna do it, they wanna do it for publicity."

Around the time of our conversation, Jay-Z declared his retirement, claiming boredom with rap music and a lack of inspiration from the hiphop world on a whole. André 3000 (who said in early 2004, "Hiphop is dead right now— honestly, that's my opinion of it."), dealing with his own ennui over rap wackness, chose to sing and play instruments through the majority of *The Love Below*, his half of the Album of the Year Grammy-winning OutKast double album, rather than solely emcee—a road also tread by Lauryn Hill, Common, Mos Def, John Forté, Cee-Lo, Wyclef Jean, Queen Latifah, and Q-Tip. The one element of hiphop pushed to the forefront for its moneymaking capability has become stale and uninventive enough that even MCs are taking issue. Innovation and excellence flourish on the fringes, but underground acts like Planet Asia, Little Brother, Jean Grae, and Madlib go unnoticed and unappreciated by mainstream radio and, by extension, listeners and record buyers.

"Back in the day, at least there was a more broad spectrum in hiphop," says Phanor. "You could enjoy a lot of different stuff. But now it's like you're force-fed one type of music and nothing else gets to break in. Honestly, if they played different stuff, people would get into it. They just don't play it. They don't even give it a chance. It's like they're force-feeding the same thing all of the time so that's what you want to hear all of the time. The radio controls everything."

Nothing succeeds like success.

4. ?UESTLOVE: *"I believe that one day when hiphop gets pregnant and has a baby, she will have offspring that will drive her just as crazy and it will be the same cycle all over again."*

It's ten o'clock—do you know where your culture is? Hiphop lives on, but most of the MCs creating novel work languish on independent record labels incapable of attracting a mass audience through radio and video networks, resigned to the fate of trees in a forest with no one to hear them fall. Commerce has gone a long way toward dulling the cutting-edge quality of rap. Music created for restrictive radio playlists is born formulaic out of necessity because, paradoxically, MCs cannot hope to sell records (and make money for themselves and their record companies) without airplay. Materialism, nihilism, social apathy—these ills stand out in bas-relief against musical backdrops that are mediocre in comparison to hiphop's golden age.

The rebellious B-boy stance loses its menace when kowtowing and conforming for regular radio rotation. Hiphop began as a counterculture and slowly evolved into the mainstream. If it's not a force of rebellion, does hiphop defeat its original purpose? At the Pink Tea Cup in Greenwich Village, as we navigate a game of Scrabble with the brainy and attractive Feigenbaum twins, the Roots drummer Ahmir Thompson a/k/a ?uestlove says, "I don't think it defeats its purpose, because it also serves as a way to empower people in today's society. In other words, Jay-Z has used hiphop to now become a successful millionaire, thus enabling people to work and get jobs. And hiphop still has this mentality of putting your peoples on. So as a result, I think that even though it doesn't serve the purpose of being the voice of the voiceless, it's now just a stepping stone for the voiceless to become the voice."

Mos Def began his debut album saying, "*People talk about hiphop like it's some giant living in the hillside coming down to visit the townspeople. We are hiphop . . . So if hiphop is about the people and hiphop won't get better until the people get better, then how do people get better?*" While all the profits of the 1988 "Self Destruction" single were donated to the National Urban League, no such beneficence came in the wake of the 2002 murder of DJ Jam Master Jay.

?uestlove says, "At this rate there is no community. Nobody gives a fuck. Motherfuckers' whole steez is, 'Yo, I'm trying to eat, trying to get a Benz, rock Evisu jeans, and get treated nice at the VIP.' I think once people come to the realization of how bullshit hiphop is . . . unless people absolutely care about the situation, I don't think that the climate will be productive or go but so far. I don't think that it can be saved. I think it's too late to turn now, and I think people just need to realize the mistakes of the past. There will be another culture that, much to our chagrin, our children will grasp onto. My ideas are strictly how to put a Band-Aid over a bullet wound."

As within, so without. Scars of the soul are why kids wear bandages when they don't have bruises. Art and culture reflect the spirit of the people, and if a breakdown is noticeable on the surface, then the inside needs healing. The urban community speaks intraculturally through hiphop, and if material excess, violence, and hedonism are dominant topics, then these are issues the community is grappling with right now. Critics of the culture would do well to deal with its illnesses—with compassion—rather than merely bitch about the symptoms. Paraphrasing muMs, hiphop could become one of the most important cultural movements of all time, second only to theology. If it fails to survive its own success, that onus may fall on the next progression of black culture.

"Once Common personified hiphop as a woman, that's how I began to look at hiphop," says ?uestlove, foreshadowing the coming of the next culture. "If you look at it in the human form as I did, then you can see where it's gonna go. It was in the womb; the nine months of the womb were all the breakbeats that came before it. Its birth in '79 with 'Rapper's Delight' . . .

"Then think of its phases. A very simplistic, 'always having fun' thing in its first five years. Think of a five-year-old; always wants to have fun and moving around crazy. I take the crack phase of it from '86 on as its first sign of seriousness. And it experimented, was curious about certain things. Think of the Bomb Squad experimenting. Puberty, discovering body parts it never had before as it grows up. Hiphop, I mean, it was fun, it was about sleepovers. Think of all the things in your childhood when you was twelve, thirteen, fourteen, fifteen. It was fun. You didn't have no caring.

"Then you went to college one day and you got a little mature. You discovered yourself, you discovered culture, you got more educated. Hiphop went through that. And hiphop didn't do everything right. Hiphop got drunk occasionally; hiphop got fucked up, got high. Motherfuckers ran a train on hiphop, hiphop got pregnant, hiphop had a few abortions: 'hip-house.' There was a few missteps. Hiphop did interracial dating with a few white boys. Hiphop graduated and became an adult.

"And once you're an adult, you can't have sleepovers and you can't stay up all night and you can't jump on your mattress and have carefree fun like you used to when you was twelve and thirteen. You gotta raise your children, you're an adult, you live in an apartment on your own. You live in a dangerous-ass neighborhood, you might have some beef with somebody, you gotta protect yourself, you gotta beat some motherfuckers down sometimes. And hiphop just wasn't as fun as an adult as it was as a kid.

"So right now, I honestly see hiphop as a twenty-five-year-old female. You know, hiphop is the youngest child of blues. Blues and gospel got married, had a rock 'n' roll son. I see jazz like a woman who couldn't pass in the States, got rejected by her own people, had to go over to Europe. After twenty-five, you're not in college no more. You are now an adult. So hiphop needs to get married. Hiphop needs to fall in love, get married, and have some children.

"And these children are gonna drive her crazy."

THE AMERICAN DREAM DICTATES that you graduate from college, do your part for the economy by joining the workforce in some corporation that keeps the system running, get married, and buy a home in the suburbs to raise your children. Hiphop upended that fantasy. Over the past thirty years hiphop has invented a new matrix by which people of color who perhaps never attended college (or even completed high school) established their own companies, becoming millionaires without conforming to the Wasp style of corporate America, making money by trading in the commodity of black culture. MCs only reap a small percentage of the overall profit generated by their music, just like their counterparts in the pop, rock, and R&B genres of the recording industry, but rhyming is a viable way to manifest wealth for many who might once have pursued illegal means to do so. Many DJs—DJ Premier, Marley Marl, and DJ Jazzy Jeff among them—became record producers and attained riches. Hiphop has spawned publications, clothing companies, music videos, television shows, literature, motion pictures, restaurants, music studios, artwork, theatre, and dance choreography providing untold opportunities for people of color whose options would have been severely limited in a previous age. Our walk, our talk, our dress, our very attitudes are marketed, promoted, and sold largely by us for the very first time in history. This is the predominant legacy of hiphop culture.

Purists see the purpose of hiphop as positive community uplift, reflected in the park jams of the seventies. Emceeing as affirmative poetry stands antithetical to street reportage on nihilistic environments, so purists will never be happy about gangsta narratives. The key is balancing the two, but radio stations don't care to help provide that balance. Modern radio cares about radio advertising, and the music playlists are more incidental than might be immediately apparent. Balance in hiphop music does exist but, unfortunately, the positive must be sought out. Supporting independent radio (as well as Internet broadcasting) and independent record labels is a good step; the major radio and record company outlets will exist in their current forms only as long as they receive public support. This has been stated time and again, yet the audience of nationwide radio increases annually, playing hiphop that purists hate for its possibly debilitating effect on their communities. Mainstream radio and video networks do not prioritize the community; they prioritize ratings.

Speculationists perceive how hiphop created a lifestyle alternative for the have-nots to survive and thrive in society, overtaking the international youth culture in the process, and expect it to expand even further. Hiphop burst forth from the Bronx to serve a cultural imperative. How is that imperative best furthered in 2004, the thirtieth anniversary of Afrika Bambaataa declaring hiphop the umbrella of the four elements? The Universal Zulu Nation advocates peace, unity, love, and having fun. KRS-One's Temple of Hiphop promotes health, love, awareness, and wealth. Russell Simmons's

Hiphop Summit Action Network endorses a fifteen-point agenda including the repealing of capital-punishment laws and the elimination of poverty. I, personally, would like the hiphop nation to embrace independent thinking and educate ourselves on spiritual principles underlying the dogma of organized religion. The time for one leader (Garvey, King, X) is antiquated; messiahs are passé—it's all too easy for that one leader to be silenced through assassination and his movement dismantled. The twenty-first century calls for a multitude of self-actualized pocket leaders, a hiphop civilization operating through a system of governance the world may never have seen before. Until then, get money.

No, seriously, I can go on, and I will because I really want this chapter to top five thousand words. How about some quotations?

"Where are the visionaries? The artists who live to advance this ancient-to-the-future African art form *and* the cause of black people at the same time? When hiphop can't be sold like fast food, maybe a revitalized underground will emerge again."

—Greg Tate

"[T]he world as I understood it no longer existed. If I was to work again at all, it would be necessary for me to come to terms with disorder."

—Joan Didion

"We cannot think of ourselves, I think, as belonging to a golden age or even a renaissance. But if we can deal with the conundrums that face us now, people later may think of us as having begun a renaissance or even a golden age."

—James Baldwin

ANOTHER GREAT DAY IN HARLEM

TWO-THIRTY P.M. Tuesday, September 29, 1998: Approaching the twenty-first century, Harlem remains the capital of black America. Barely three weeks after the polemical Million Youth March spearheaded by Minister Khallid Muhammad, Uptown adds another historical event to her lifespan this sunlit afternoon. Within the next five minutes, at 17 East One Hundred Twenty-sixth Street, a momentous portrait for the posterity of hiphop culture will be captured for the ages to come.

Excitement and expectancy brew on this barricaded block between Madison and Fifth Avenue a/k/a National Black Theatre Way. Hiphop dignitaries like Kool DJ Herc, the Goodie Mob, Rakim, Eightball & MJG, and E-40 take their places on the steps of three brownstones, two stately edifices bracketing the dilapidated stoop in the center. "Out of respect for Mr. Parks, if you're not an artist, would you please step away from the shoot?" asks Def Jam Recordings cofounder Russell Simmons, dressed in a sleeveless argyle Phat Farm sweater with sweatpants and backwards baseball cap, speaking through a megaphone. Having lent an impromptu organizational helping hand, he returns the bullhorn to *XXL* magazine publisher Dennis Page, who continues to impose order on the proceedings. Legendary octogenarian photojournalist Gordon Parks lingers across the street between two tripod-supported cameras; he soft-spokenly commands a small crew of assistants. Directed by his pipe-wielding right hand, the amorphous assortment of over one hundred hiphop personalities takes shape. "It'd be nice if they put some music with it," says an onlooking middle-aged female Harlem resident, leaning out a window. Shots are taken, history is made.

Then, slowly approaching the yearbook photo–styled congregation from stage left, the right man arrives at the right time. The crowd, which already includes such hiphop heavy-hitters as Grandmaster Flash, Slick Rick, and DJ Hollywood, breaks out into resounding applause. Coasting on his fat-laced Adidas, dipped in a black Phat Farm sweat-shirt and jeans with a fedora, is none other than Joseph "Run" Simmons, who briskly takes his place in the center of the throng beside his older brother Russell. A classic hiphop moment.

FORTY YEARS AGO, eccentric jazz pianist Thelonious Monk exhausted over an hour deciding what to wear to a noonish photo shoot in Harlem, organized by *Esquire* art director Art Kane. Eventually electing to go with a light-colored sports jacket (so as to better stand out in a crowd of dark-colored suits), Monk cabbed a ride with alto saxophonist Gigi Gryce and Riverside Records publicist Robert Altshular. The late Art Kane's concept was to assemble the most notable jazz musicians of the day to pose for the January 1959 issue of *Esquire* on the steps of a brownstone on One Hundred Twenty-sixth Street. Through a combination of considered orchestration and word of mouth, fifty-seven players—including Charles Mingus, Count Basie, and Dizzy Gillespie—showed for the historic gathering that resulted in *Jazz Portrait*, a photo hanging in black neighborhood barbershops and numbers spots to this day. "In the jazz age," says Fugees founding father Wyclef Jean, "you had Thelonious Monk, Charlie Parker. In the hiphop age, you got Wu-Tang Clan, Fugees, Master P. What those musics have in common is freedom of expression. In its rawest form, it wasn't meant to be sold. It was made just to be heard as a feeling. Like you have a Canibus or a Nas. That's equivalent to Charlie Parker doing his chops on the sax. It's just a new era."

The era captured in *Jazz Portrait* was fleshed out in that same issue of *Esquire* in an essay written by John Clellon Holmes. In his 1952 novel *Go*, Holmes captured the flavor of the Beat generation—whose preoccupations were directly guided by jazz and the fifties black aesthetic—five years before writer Jack Kerouac defined the movement with *On the Road*. Holmes used his position as a precursor to the Beats to assume the role of their chief chronicler. According to his *Esquire* article, three things are necessary to constitute a golden age: an audience, a tradition, and an aesthetic. Though the golden age of hiphop culture is generally presumed to have taken place somewhere between Run-D.M.C.'s 1984 self-titled debut and Dr. Dre's 1992 *The Chronic*, the modern climate of 1998 is rife with evidence of a resurgence. "This is the biggest year of Def Jam, or the biggest year of rap," says Russell Simmons. "I'm sure the numbers at the end of the year will tally up and be bigger than they were ever before, and every year it's been doing that pretty much. Peaking."

Hiphop as a culture, at the crest of the twenty-first century, is widely considered a given. In the fifties, declaring jazz an art form seemed a rather audacious statement for a mainstream American publication to make. "Never in the history of man's need to express himself in song has half a century sufficed to transform a folk music into an art music," wrote

Holmes. During the past forty years, however, the rapid pace of change has accelerated this process. Would anyone argue against the lasting significance of rock, punk, or reggae music? Back before the commercial breakthrough of the Sugarhill Gang's "Rapper's Delight," the audience for hiphop was confined to New York City and its immediate environs. Over twenty years later, hiphop is an international force, with MCs like Takagi Kan from Japan and France's MC Solaar representing well. Hiphop has long since expanded its following, from packing the local Bronx nightclubs of the Funhouse and the Disco Fever to selling out stadiums like Madison Square Garden and the Pontiac Silverdome.

"The thing I believe separates hiphop culture from the jazz is that twenty years later, it's still being solidified and reaffirmed as a youth culture," observes Russell Simmons. "Instead of hiphop music growing up with its audience, it splintered off. It's still about rebelling; it's still about changing society. That's what gives rap an even longer foothold in the mainstream, in terms of sales. The jazz guys were cool, [but] they never change. The thing is, when you get the politicians twenty years later still making comments about how obscene, aggressive, or counterculture these artists are, it just keeps affirming its presence as the voice of the youth. And that's what makes it special."

The most striking observation, especially in the wake of the deaths of 2Pac and the Notorious B.I.G., is the current all-world nature of the hiphop audience. Millions of listeners nationwide get excited by Georgia's OutKast, Missouri's Nelly, and Eminem of Michigan. Whereas allegiances once bandied strictly between New York and California—with an occasional Geto Boys (Texas) or 2 Live Crew (Florida) getting love—the hiphop audience has now become as nonpartisan as ever, at a time when the hiphop nation is at its most unified. Solidarity in hiphop was the major impetus for *XXL* celebrating the fortieth anniversary of *Jazz Portrait* with a coming together of hiphop's major cultural icons. "This little function right here is showing the fact that everybody's cool with everybody," says Jermaine Dupri, hours before the photo is taken. "It's starting to look like the same thing [as the jazz age], just done in a younger, youthful type of fashion."

In 1995, shots rang out over video production trailers in Red Hook, Brooklyn, on the set of Tha Dogg Pound's "New York, New York" video. Snoop Dogg, Daz Dillinger, and Kurupt took the hint and swiftly broke camp back to Long Beach, California. Now signing autographs on the steps of the Metropolitan Community Methodist Church three years later—one week before his solo double-album, *Kuruption*, debuted in the pop Top Ten of the *Billboard* magazine chart—Kurupt bathes in completely different vibes. "Niggas'll kill over hiphop," he explains. "They'll argue and damn near fight over who they think is the best and who's not, so you know it's from the heart. And with jazz, it's from their hearts. We've been at this struggle for a long time. Hiphop is like a race. Like the fight blacks had to get in the level they are, that's the fight that we had to get where we are."

Crowds for the House of Blues–sponsored Smokin Grooves tour (in which Gang Starr, Public Enemy, and the Refugee Allstars took it to the stage), in addition to A Tribe Called Quest's farewell outing with the Beastie Boys, reinforce the viability of the hiphop audience and recall concert packages that hearken back to the Fresh Fest and Run-D.M.C./Beastie Boys bills of old. Grassroots hiphop purist artists like Mos Def and Talib Kweli have also been able to maximize their underground buzz by hitting the nightclub circuit for successful one-nighters.

If international eminence, nationwide style pollination, and reaching the concert masses all indicate that hiphop commands its most eager audience ever, recent bids to court an even wider mainstream America cannot be ignored. P. Diddy featuring former Led Zeppelin guitarist Jimmy Page on "Come with Me"? Method Man with Limp Bizkit on "N 2 Gether Now"? The lengthy list also includes "The Omen" with DMX and Marilyn Manson. Such alliances go back as far as Afrika Bambaataa's 1984 "World Destruction" collaboration with John Lydon, but these developments say as much about the expanded hiphop fanbase as do the magazines devoted entirely to hiphop. The culture now reaches millions more than during its previous golden age.

EVER HEAR WU-TANG CLAN flip Run-D.M.C.'s "Sucker M.C.'s (Krush-Groove 1)" from *In the Beginning . . . There Was Rap*? How about Foxy Brown's "Rock the Bells" rendition (originally recorded by LL Cool J), "Foxy's Bells," or that N.W.A tribute cover album? All these efforts are evidence of a respect for the past and an emerging sense of tradition, John Clellon Holmes's second attribute of a golden age. "A lot of artists just skip over hiphop and go to rap," says the Jungle Brothers' Afrika Baby Bam, discussing the nuances of hiphop traditionalism. "It's been dissected. Rap is just the commercial part that the industry uses to sell the product. The hiphop aspect of it started fifteen, twenty years ago. And that's like a tidal wave. If you wasn't there when it was getting ready to rise and groom you, then you just missed when it splashed and went back to sea. And now, what you have is just the sand—you just have rap. A lot of artists come up and they don't even have their feet wet."

With the nostalgic popularity of tracks like the Def Squad's "Rapper's Delight," connecting the dots between old school (Disco King Mario) and new school (DJ Q-bert) has gotten easier. "[Hiphoppers] have the opportunity to jump into the water, study it, and learn what it is," continues

Afrika Baby Bam. "What's the tangible thing that makes them an artist, and what makes their art form a craft? All that is out there to get access to. For the most part, I think jazz artists stayed more into their culture because there's less of a commercial inclination."

Many in hiphop circa 1993 were damn near disturbed to hear Snoop Dogg's inimitable drawl interpreting Slick Rick's 1985 classic, "La Di Da Di." Covering rap material took nearly twenty years to become acceptable, partly because of the very personal creative process involved in emceeing (poet Jessica Care Moore would not recite verses by Ursula Rucker, or vice versa), but also because in hiphop, time and knowledge have just recently melded enough to constitute tradition. Rap is now replete with the likes of Buckshot's "I Ain't No Joke" (Rakim), Snoop Dogg's "Vapors" (Biz Markie), and Rampage's "Flipmode Enemy #1" (Public Enemy), all testaments to a respect for the past. With the release of Rhino Records compilations like *Fat Beats & Brastraps* and *Kurtis Blow Presents Hiphop Classics*, younger MCs can profit from exposure to the tradition they will inherit. A greater awareness allows for an up-and-coming rapper like Harlem World's Cardan to find and flaunt the latent Southern booty boogie bounce in Newcleus's "Jam on It."

THE HIPHOP AESTHETIC—principles of the culture adhered to at a given time—is open to a widening of possibilities, powered by the questionable prominence of materialism. "Jazz players, most of them wasn't getting money like that," remarks Fat Joe. "It wasn't a money thing. It was more [about] the art. They wanted to express themselves through their music. As far as hiphop, it's turned into a moneymaking machine where people are more interested in the monies they could make. You still have certain people preserving the hiphop culture. It's not a bad thing, 'cause it means more black people getting money." Wyclef Jean adds, "Rappers get paid. Most jazz musicians died broke."

The aesthetic revolution to transform hiphop most dramatically was the dual financial and artistic success of Death Row Records in the early nineties. Though Herbie Hancock's *Head Hunters* and Miles Davis's *Kind of Blue* stand as the only multiplatinum-selling releases in jazz history, hiphop albums were now expected to sell competitively with pop music in the wake of consistent platinum-plus creations like *The Chronic*, *Doggystyle*, and *Above the Rim*. This dubious expectation has inevitably resulted in many sacrifices of artistry for commerce—as it does in pop—but also opens doors for hiphop experimentalists who would not have been blessed with record deals at an earlier stage. Experimental artists like Tricky, DJ Spooky, Goldie, even the more traditional RZA and the Roots, are all beneficiaries of the modern hiphop aesthetic, where creative improvisation has been given a forum due partially to the financial success of mainstream hiphop. "Everybody don't have to rhyme the same way to blow or talk about the same thing to get recognition," says microphone legend Rakim. "You'll find brothers coming out doing that abstract, crazy [material]. People are scared to go left, but myself, I'ma do it anyway. I came out and went against the grain."

NEW POSSIBILITIES AND NEW OPPORTUNITIES exist in this hiphop renaissance and, paraphrasing John Clellon Holmes's 1958 prediction for jazz, the next twenty years are certain to be more incredible than the last. "Today, I think, was the day hiphop was seriously validated," says the Roots' drummer Ahmir Thompson in September 1998, recording the manic activity on One Hundred Twenty-sixth Street with a handheld camcorder. Last night the Roots completed mastering on *Things Fall Apart*; today, they partake in what *XXL*'s cover tagline calls "hiphop on a higher level." "More than any-thing, it's like the Million Man Hiphoppers. I just got over-whelmed. From me not even having to introduce myself to Rakim to seeing Deborah Harry, Kool Herc, Kangol from UTFO. Everyone knows how gung-ho crazy I am about hiphop just in general. I'm a kid in a candy store."

So many stories, so many surreal tableaux. Jermaine Dupri and Grandmaster Flash. Pee Wee Dance and Busta Rhymes. Fab 5 Freddy and Special K. DJ Jazzy Jeff and Q-Tip. The Jungle Brothers and De La Soul. D'Angelo administering handclasps to the hiphop cognoscenti while singer Angie Stone (p/k/a MC Angie B of Sequence) cradles their corn-rowed one-year-old son Michael D'Angelo Archer II across the street. Come three forty-five, the police insist on dis-persing the hundreds gathered, but the positive vibes extend throughout the afternoon. "I'm just happy to be here to be a part of this," reflects De La Soul's Pos, wiping sweat from his brow. "Us being youths, doing our thing, and just trying to create all types of levels of music from all different back-grounds is the same way jazz did. We're collaging our feelings with understanding where we come from. There's definitely a parallel."

ACKNOWLEDGMENTS

Mom • Dad • Grandma Neet • Grandma & Grandpa Benton, Grandma & Grandpa Johnson, Grandma Greene—thanks for your help, truly • Kyle M. Lewis • Christopher M. Lewis • Craig M. Lewis • Sheldon Benton • Barbara Futrell • Juanda M. Lewis-Morton • Javonne M. A. Singleton • Jazmine M. Lewis • Janeé M. Lewis • Carl Benton • Charles Joyner • Janine Porterfield • Jason Futrell • Jonathan Rivera • Justice Martinez • Epperson • M. Aleijuan King • David T. Muhammad • Dinkinish O'Connor • Cissine • Charmaine Crawford • Elsa Mehary • Reginald & Melinda Lewis • Michael A. Gonzales • *ego trip* Monkey Academy • Fahiym Ratcliffe & Goddess Imani Jones • Emma & Zoë Feigenbaum • N'Gai Slader • Kerisha Hicks • Jay Weaver • John Muhammad • muMs (thanks for the pretentious title, keep scheming) • Johnny Temple, thanks so much for setting this off • Johanna Ingalls • my agent Anna Ghosh & Scovil Chichak Galen • my lawyer Julian Riley Esq. • Lionel Phillips & Bunnymerce Bernard • Mrs. Judith Krutoy—for Camus, Sartre & Morrison at sixteen • The Alpha Posse: Reg Johnson, Mike Jones, Derrick Sibert, Reg Peoples, Art Brown, John Thomas, Dave Horace • The Sagittarius Posse: Richard Pryor, Joan Didion, Gordon Parks, Jimi Hendrix, Woody Allen, John F. Kennedy Jr., Steven Spielberg, Jay-Z, Jim Morrison, Mos Def, Bruce Lee, Frank Sinatra, Lester Bangs, Walt Disney, Charles M. Schulz • Darling Nikki Smith • Caille Millner • Basheera James • Robert Christgau & Chuck Eddy @ *The Village Voice* • John Payne @ *L.A. Weekly* • Nathan Brackett @ *Rolling Stone* • N'Dambi (for asking about "the book" since '97) & Shani Zafin • E. Badu • P. T. Anderson • hiphop & the Bronx, without which there's no book • Marvel & DC Comics, Jack "King" Kirby, Stan "The Man" Lee, Frank Miller, John Byrne, George Pérez ("South Bronx, South South Bronx"), Marv Wolfman, Steve Ditko, Jim Steranko, Bill Sienkiewicz • Prince • Tyge, Mr. Mills, M-Love, Christian Max, Trophy, Butch M. Lewis & MML-Ski • and most importantly, my readers

Also from **AKASHIC BOOKS**

LIMBO by Sean Keith Henry
270 pages, a trade paperback original, $15.95
ISBN: 1-888451-55-6
"*Limbo* is a smart, honest novel about displacement and the meaning of home. It struggles in turn with the embracing of identity and the welcome comfort of escape."
—PERCIVAL EVERETT, author of *Erasure*, winner of the Hurston/Wright Legacy Award

"*Limbo* is a strong, unsettling novel about race, dislocation, and the fragility of human connection. Through a series of events that seem both startling and inevitable, it skillfully depicts the ways we become alienated from those who love us—and from ourselves."
—NINA REVOYR, author of *Southland*

R&B (RHYTHM & BUSINESS):
THE POLITICAL ECONOMY OF BLACK MUSIC
edited by Norman Kelley
338 pages, hardcover, $24.95
ISBN: 1-888451-26-2
"Seminal rapper Chuck D of Public Enemy once asked the musical question, 'Who stole the soul?' In this anthology, perhaps the first to deal solely with the business of black music, Chuck D, editor Kelley, and other name contributors (including Courtney Love) attempt to come up with some answers. The history of the modern recording industry is dissected in several eyeopening contributions that should be required reading for anyone interested in popular music."
—*Library Journal*

A PHAT DEATH by Norman Kelley
A Nina Halligan Mystery
260 pages, a trade paperback original, $14.95
ISBN: 1-888451-48-3
"Nina Halligan takes on the recording industry and black music in Norman Kelley's third outrageous caper to feature the bad girl PI . . . Once again outspoken social criticism fires the nonstop action."
—*Publishers Weekly*